# A Look into the
# Rear View Mirror

Carolyn Noah Graetz

authorHOUSE®

*AuthorHouse™*
*1663 Liberty Drive*
*Bloomington, IN 47403*
*www.authorhouse.com*
*Phone: 1-800-839-8640*

*First published by AuthorHouse    09/20/2011*

*ISBN: 978-1-4634-4462-4 (sc)*
*ISBN: 978-1-4634-4461-7 (ebk)*

*Library of Congress Control Number: 2011914168*

*Printed in the United States of America*

# Dedication

To my children, Derek and Gionne Graetz and to my nephews and nieces, Douglas Planer and Susan Planer Phillips, Duane "Tally" Noah and Holley Noah, who most likely will not grasp the work that has gone into writing this book until it is too late to discuss it. But hopefully one day they all will read and have a greater understanding of their mother's and aunt's life growing up as a country girl in the rural part of her beloved state of Mississippi, and what a life-changing event occurred when she entered nursing school in New Orleans. To all of them I dedicate this book.

Make me always ready
to come to you with clean hands
and straight eyes, so when life fades
as a sunset, my spirit
will come to you without shame

Lakota Indian prayer

# "When Dogwoods Bloom in Mississippi"

When Dogwoods bloom in Mississippi,

When the shadows of these blossoms
Add their beauty to the night.

When Dogwoods bloom in Mississippi
With their blossoms white and rare
I'll be coming home to visit
For my heart is ever there.

When Dogwoods bloom in Mississippi,
And the song of night birds fills the air;
When the trees are turning green,
With joy in my heart, I'll be there.

When Dogwoods bloom in Mississippi,
And Whippoorwills call at night;
When Mockingbirds sing at dawn,
I'll be listening with delight.

When Dogwoods bloom in Mississippi,
And there is ever a song in the air;
When Bluebirds and Robins are nesting,
I promise, I'll be there!

Lynn Stone Armstrong
September 1940

# Acknowledgements

When one writes a book it is difficult to know where to begin with whom you want to thank. There are too many folks to name all of the names. However, many of the names are included in the book, and I want to thank them very much for their contributions. They are my siblings, my aunts, my cousins, and many of my nursing school classmates. They are all mentioned in the book, and I am happy that they are and have been a part of my life.

To write a book for publication one needs encouragement. In February 2002 at the Cottonlandia Museum in Greenwood, Mississippi, I mentioned that I was writing a book about my ancestry and about my family in Carroll County. A member of the Friends of Cottonlandia encouraged me to let them know when the book was completed.

Later that year I attended Jimmy Johnson's funeral in Lexington, Mississippi. Jimmy was a frequent visitor to the public library there. I mentioned to Laura Lawson, the librarian, at the Lexington Library that I was writing a book about my family's life in Carroll County, Mississippi. She invited me to come for a book signing at the Lexington Library.

A number of my nursing school classmates and other friends have given me encouragement to write and have contributed to this book. For that encouragement, I am grateful.

Roger Graetz, my husband of forty-six years, I owe a special thanks too for making this book possible. Without you making copies of old photographs and helping me with the photo placements in this book, and without the computer skills you have taught me over the years I could not have written this book.

A special thanks to Gary Michael Smith, author of *Publishing for Small Press Runs*. I took a non-credit course from him at the University of New Orleans in 2001 using his book as a resource. But what I have gotten from Gary goes above and beyond the call of duty. He gave us his e-mail address, and I continue to e-mail Gary with questions. He always responds to my questions in less than twenty-four hours. I am a lucky person, I know it and I feel it, meeting Gary Michel Smith has added to that luck dimension. Thank you, Gary.

Thanks also to Marie Jeanne Trauth, my editor, for the advice and for the funny comments.

Thanks to Jan DiCicco, a Toastmaster friend, for volunteering to do a second editing. She is a tough editor and I am grateful for her friendship and her skills.

Let me not forget Amelie Welman, Administrative Assistance, at the Lakeview Presbyterian in New Orleans, Louisiana who bravely did some last minute editing.

A book is really a team effort and I do thank all who made a contribution to this book.

Books that I had earlier printed were lost to Hurricane Katrina. and the aftermath of its flood waters which caused the 17th Street Canal levee to break in New Orleans, Louisiana on August 29, 2005. Several folks have asked for books therefore another printing.

# Contents

# Introduction

How dear to my heart
memories of days gone by
this book breathing new life

The original purpose of writing this book was to share written information with my progeny. I wanted to share words and pictures that celebrate my life and the life of my family growing up in the rural part of Mississippi.

I wanted them to be able to read, look back, and understand from what place their mother came. With this purpose in mind it is my hope that the information in this book will serve as a tool to connect my progeny to their ancestors, to their heritage, and to value both.

It is, also, my desire that they will be open, attentive, and willing to use their time, talents and considerable intellect to expand their minds in many and varied ways, formal or informal, all the days of their lives. For the most part it is a personal history and this history helps me and I hope future generations to look into the rear view mirror and see what life was like.

A huge turning point in my life began on September 4, 1956, when I entered nursing school at the Touro Infirmary School of Nursing in New Orleans, Louisiana. I was a student nurse there from that date in September 1956 until September 3, 1959. I have made an effort to reconstruct that past experience.

The greater portion of what is written are my own memories, you might call them flashes, happy and unhappy, from my memory bank. At times I pressed my own memory button, and one thing came to mind and at other times a topic would come to my mind when I was talking with someone.

In so many ways I consider myself as having been born lucky with many blessings. The fact that I was born in the United States of America with good health must be acknowledged. I had two parents who lived until I was in my late fifties. I have four siblings and that is a wonderful blessing. I had the blessing of knowing all four of my grandparents and only one of them died before I was in my twenties.

I was born into a family that was disciplined to work and expected to do so. I was brought up with a belief in God, and I grew up knowing the importance of helping others. For all of these blessings I am thankful.

There have been hardships in my life, too. Having first hand experience with hardships has given me a heightened sensitivity to the sufferings of others. Perhaps some of these adversities have illuminated my path in the world so that I have a greater understanding of others, and I have become a more empathetic person toward others who are experiencing adversities in life.

For the most part I feel that adversities and hardships have been learning experiences, which have made me a better, stronger and wiser person. For this reason, perhaps I can be thankful for the adversities in my life.

All through the narrative portion of the book you will come across historical highlights that generally follow information about that person or those persons who were discussed in the previous chapter of the book.

As you, the reader, wade through these collected and recollected memories I encourage you to take time to enjoy the journey, a journey back in time.

Carolyn Sue Noah Graetz
2004

# Chapter 1   Ancestral Background

From Scotland, Ireland, England and Germany to the United States, from Pennsylvania, Maryland, Alabama, Virginia, Tennessee, North Carolina, and South Carolina my ancestors came to Mississippi.

Those coming from Scotland, Ireland, and England were colonists searching for freedom. They did not gain freedom immediately as those early colonies were governed by England. But some of the colonists were discontented as British citizens, and this discontent led to the Revolutionary War. Some of my ancestors were participants in that war.

Confirmed ancestors involved in the Revolutionary War are Gilbert Johnstone II and John Caffey. Gilbert Johnstone, whose ancestral land was Scotland, was born in Armaugh, Ireland, in 1725. He was among the many Scots-Irish who left Ireland for the colonies of North America.

**Oakwood Cemetery**
**Montgomery, Alabama**

**Carolyn Noah Graetz at Tomb of John Caffey**

From 1776 to 1780, Gilbert and his eldest son, Hugo, organized and equipped a company of Partisan Horse and led them under Folsome in North Carolina. From 1780 to 1783 they were under Francis Marion in South Carolina. Documentation of this can be found in the Joseph Haberstram Chapter Daughters of the American Revolution Historical Collection 1902 Volume I page 14, 15, article by Huger Johnson.

John Caffey was the son of Michael Caffey, who was born in Belfast, Ireland. John, however, was born on the Eastern Shore of Maryland. He served with Sixth Maryland Independent Company. At various times in the Revolutionary War he served under General George Washington and Lafayette. This data is on his tombstone in the Oakwood Cemetery Montgomery, Alabama.

Both Gilbert Johnstone and John Caffey are ancestors of my paternal great grandmother, Annie Johnson, who married Jesse Shull Randall.

My ancestral connection to both follows:

Gilbert Johnstone II married Margaret Warburton
Their son, Gilbert Johnstone III, married a Mary (surname unknown)

Their son, Samuel Johnson (unknown when spelling of name change, but at the time of his marriage to Patsy, it is Johnson), married Patsy Collier

Their son, Gilbert Johnson, married Emily Blakely

Their daughter, Annie Johnson, married Jesse Shull Randall

Their daughter, Willie Mae Randall, married Thomas Anderson Noah

Their son, Robert Randall Noah, married Susie Evelyn "Dollie" Mann

Their daughter, I, Carolyn Sue Noah Graetz, is this book's author and this accounts for the lineage, which granted me eligibility into the Daughters of the American Revolution.

1776        1890

THE NATIONAL SOCIETY OF THE

# Daughters of the American Revolution

This certifies that

## Carolyn Sue Noah Graetz

is a regularly approved member of the National Society of the Daughters of the American Revolution, having been admitted by the National Board of Management by virtue of her descent from a patriot who with unfailing loyalty served as a sailor, soldier, civil officer, or rendered material aid to the cause of American Independence during the Revolutionary War.

Given under our hands and the seal of the National Society this      seventh      day of   June     19 97

National No.   0778746

Admitted    June 7, 1997

Ancestor:   Gilbert Johnstone SR
South Carolina

_Norla E. Kemper_
President General

_Marylean F. Wight_
Recording Secretary General

_Lynda Tyzika Watkins_
Registrar General

Gilbert Johnstone Revolutionary War Veteran
in Scots Archery Uniform 1745

John Caffey's connection to me is as follows:

John Caffey married Mary Buchanan

Their son, Henry Caffey, married Lavinia Thompson

Their daughter, Elizabeth Caffey, married Ellis/Eli Blakely

Their daughter, Emily Blakely, married Gilbert Johnson
*Note this Gilbert Johnson was the great grandson of Gilbert Johnstone II above.

Their daughter, Annie Johnson, married Jesse Shull Randall

Their daughter, Willie Mae Randall, married Thomas Anderson Noah

Their son, Robert Randall Noah, married Susie Evelyn "Dollie" Mann

Their daughter, I, Carolyn Sue Noah Graetz, placed this information into this book. However, I credit much of my research to a second cousin once removed, Jimmy Johnson.

My earliest recorded ancestors in Mississippi were the Johnsons and Colliers who arrived in Warren County, Mississippi, in the early 1800s. The Johnstons (later Johnson) migrated from South Carolina around 1815, and the Colliers came down the Mississippi River from Tennessee sometime prior to 1820 (information obtained verbally from my great uncle Dell Mann, whose mother was a niece of Patsy Collier). Their families were likely attracted to the Mississippi Delta farmland because of its rich soil, improved cottonseed, and the availability of slave labor. At that time, these factors made Mississippi one of the wealthiest states.

On January 12, 1820, Samuel Johnson and Patsy Collier were married in Warren County, Mississippi. Mississippi was in the Union for less than three years, admitted as the twentieth state on December 10, 1817. Natchez was the state capital in 1820, and the area of present day Jackson was called LeFleur's Bluff. The fifth president, James Monroe, was in office.

Samuel and Patsy later moved to Carroll County. Certainly they had an adventuresome spirit to leave a more established section of Mississippi for a primitive area that had woods with only Indian trails. Most likely Samuel and other early settlers had knowledge of these lands becoming available following the Treaty of Dancing Rabbit Creek with the Choctaw Indians.

Ancestors

stumbling in the dark

eureka

It is unknown how long the Indians were in that part of North America, but the Choctaws were found there in 1820. In September 1830, the Treaty of Dancing Rabbit Creek was signed between the United States commissioners and the Choctaws. This treaty resulted in granting all Choctaw lands east of the Mississippi River, an area of 12,000 square miles, to the United States Government.

In 1833, these lands were divided into many counties by an Act of the Mississippi Legislature. Carroll County was one of them. It was named for Charles G. Carroll of Maryland, one of the signers of the Declaration of Independence. Most of the Choctaws from this area followed the "Trail of Tears" into the Indian Territory, which is the state of Oklahoma today.

Little is known about Samuel and Patsy Johnson's life in Carroll County, but it is known that Samuel paid taxes there in 1835, proof that they were among the earliest of settlers there.

Samuel must have been a yeoman farmer, a system advocated by Thomas Jefferson, which was never realized entirely by our country. Many of Samuel's descendants, including my father's generation four generations later, became small farmers. Now there are fifth generation descendants of Samuel Johnson in Carroll County who are cotton farmers. They are my first cousins, Joe and Marion Jones, sons of my father's sister, Ruby Noah Jones.

Also, it is known that Samuel bought a slave—Joseph was his name—from Caleb Young for $600 on March 27, 1843. The document states that Joseph was thirty years old, healthy, and a slave for life. However, there is no evidence that Samuel ever owned a large plantation. He did have a big family and they were a large part of his labor force. Samuel's progeny would eventually pay a price for the institution of slavery, the original sin of the South some believe.

Other early settlers arriving in Carroll County about the same time Samuel and Patsy Johnson were Daniel McEachern and his wife Mary McDougal McEachern. In an old Presbyterian Session book at the Union Church in Jefferson County, Mississippi, it is recorded that this couple was dismissed to Carroll County, Mississippi, on June 12, 1832.

In the McEachern Family of Carroll County, Mississippi, Sally Stone Trotter wrote about Daniel and Mary McEachern settling on Bogahala Creek near the ancient Indian Village of Shongalo. They were among the charter members of the Shongalo Presbyterian Church, which was organized in 1835. The church was later moved into the town of Vaiden a couple miles from Shongalo Village.

Descendents Daniel and Mary McEachern, Helen Claire McEachern Elliot and Bob McEachern., are members of that same church today. Bob's wife Lucy is a childhood friend of mine.

Samuel's and Patsy's children were William, Gilbert "Dock," Sarah, Hugh, John, Martha, and Samuel Parsons. I descend from the line of Gilbert.

My Compton ancestors arrived early in Carroll County, also. Allen Compton, my great-grandfather, was born there in 1835; the same year that Samuel Johnson paid taxes.

One set of my mother's paternal great—grandparents, German Mann and Elmyria Ringer, were married in Clark County, Mississippi, around 1857 prior to moving to Carroll County, Mississippi. German Mann had come to that part of Mississippi from Petersburg, Virginia. Their son John Wishum Mann married Sarah Collier in Carroll County, Mississippi in 1877. This information was given to Sarah Dell Mann Bell by her father, Bertis Ledell "Dell" Mann, a son of John and Sarah Collier Mann. She provided that information in writing to me. Other written information was given to me by Bill Belt, husband of Bernice Mann Belt, and a son-in-law of Verge Mann, who was a brother of my grandfather, Floyd Mann.

It is unknown when the Randalls arrived in Carroll County, but it is known that Jesse Randall married Annie Johnson there in 1892.

My Noah ancestral line was the last to arrive in Carroll County, Mississippi. They migrated to Carroll County from Alabama in the winter of 1895. By this time our country was over one hundred years old. There were forty-four states in the United States and Grover Cleveland, the twenty-fourth president, was in office.

Samuel Parsons Johnson Confederate Civil War Veteran
with his wife Susan Eliza and children standing left to right: Thomas,
Lewis Henry, George, Joseph Emmitt, Mamie, Mattie Esther, and
small son Samuel Plunkett ** Samuel Plunkett and Joseph Emmitt are
potentially the opposite of the labeling, but was the best guess by Greg
Johnson, grandson of Joseph Emmitt. Samuel Parsons was the son of
Samuel and Patsy Collier Johnson early settlers to Carroll County.

# Chronology

| | |
|---|---|
| 1783 | Treaty of Paris-ending the Revolutionary War—was signed by the American colonies and Great Britain |
| 1793 | On September 3, 1793 President George Washington laid cornerstone of the Capital building in Washington D.C. |
| 1793 | Eli Whitney invented the cotton gin. |
| 1803 | In April 1803 President Thomas Jefferson sent James Monroe and Robert Livingston to France to attempt to purchase the "Isle of Orleans" and West Florida. Congress granted them $2 million for the purchase. But when they arrived the French foreign minister, Charles Maurice de Talleyrand, knowing that Louisiana was of diminishing importance to France, opened negotiations by asking Livingston what the United States would give for all of Louisiana. By April 29, the envoys agreed to pay a total of $15 million to France for the entire Louisiana territory. A treaty, dated April 30, 1803, was signed on May 2. That treaty was ratified by the U.S. Senate in October, and the U. S. flag was raised over New Orleans, on December 20, 1803. |
| 1804-1806 | Meriwether Lewis and William Clark left the area of St. Louis, Missouri, on May 14, 1804, searching for a Northwestern water route to the Pacific Ocean. They returned to St. Louis on September 23, 1806. They made it to the Pacific Ocean via the Missouri River, passing over the treacherous Rocky Mountains in Montana and then via the Columbia River to the Pacific Ocean. However, Lewis was disappointed with the fact that he failed to find there was, in fact, no uninterrupted water route to the Pacific. |
| 1812-1815 | War between England and the United States was caused by British interference with American trade, impressments of American seamen, and "the War Hawks"—John Calhoun, Henry Clay, and Daniel Webster—drive for western expansion. Peace Treaty of Ghent to end the war was signed late in 1814. However, the signing of this treaty was not known to General Andrew Jackson or to Sir Edward Pakenham. Hence, the Battle of New Orleans was fought after that treaty was signed. In this final battle, Andrew Jackson beat back an attack by |

the British under the leadership of Pakenham on January 8, 1815. From the American point of view, this was not a useless battle since the actual ratification of the Treaty of Ghent did not take place until February 17, 1815.

1820    Martha/Patsy Collier and Samuel Johnston were married in Warren County, Mississippi on January 12, 1820.

1820    Florence Nightingale, English nurse and founder of modern nursing, was born in Florence, Italy. Her life was dedicated to the care of the sick and war wounded. In 1844, she began to visit hospitals. In 1850, she spent some time with the nursing Sisters of St. Vincent de Paul in Alexandria, and in 1851 she studied at the Institute for Protestant Deaconesses in Kaiserwerth, Germany. It was in the Crimean War where she organized a unit of 38 women nurses and from that point in her life onward she became a legend. With funds she collected for her war services she established the Nightingale School and Home for training nurses at St. Thomas's Hospital in London in 1860. She was called "the Lady with the Lamp" because she believed that a nurse's care was never ceasing, night or day: She taught that nursing was a noble profession, and she made it so.

1820    Another headline news event in the year of Samuel and Patsy's marriage was the jailing of Napoleon Bonaparte, that great French leader and conqueror, on the isle of Corsica.

1830    Treaty of Dancing Rabbit Creek was signed between the Choctaw Indians and the United States commissioners. Greenwood LeFleur, later Leflore, the chief of the Choctaw Nation was prominent in that treaty. By the terms of the treaty he was granted a home site and several thousand acres of land in Carroll County. My ancestors would later migrate to this land of the noble Redman, who were at times referred to as blood thirsty savages.

1833    Carroll County, Mississippi, was carved out of the territory ceded by the Choctaw Indians. With most of the Choctaws out, there was in irresistible urge for white settlers to pour in to the newly opened territory. They came from Tennessee, from North and South Carolina, from Virginia, Georgia, and in the case of my ancestors they came from other places in Mississippi. In December 1833 this territory was divided into many counties with Carroll County being one of them. Carroll County was named for Charles Carroll of Maryland, one of the signers of the Declaration of Independence. At first Carroll County's size was 908 square miles but in 1870 the state legislature took parts of other counties including Carroll to form Grenada, Leflore, and Montgomery counties reducing Carroll to 615 square miles.

1835    Greenwood Leflore was sent to the Mississippi legislature as Carroll County's first representative. He later became a state senator and served from 1841-1844. Greenwood Leflore strongly opposed secession. When the United States Civil War broke out, he refused to recognize the change in government and it is written that he never accepted Confederate money.

1835    Samuel Johnson paid taxes in Carroll County, Mississippi.

1835    Shongalo Presbyterian Church was organized at Shongalo Village in Carroll County, Mississippi. Church was later moved into the town of Vaiden and remains there today.

# Chapter 2   Great-Grandparents

## Part 1: Jesse Shull Randall and Annie Johnson Randall

> Time standing still
> ancestors murmuring
> stories of yore

Part 1A: Jesse Shull Randall, my father's grandfather, was born on January 22, 1869, in Lowndes County, Mississippi. Andrew Johnson was president of the United State, but Ulysses Grant was sworn in as the eighteenth United States President that same year on March 4th.

Jesse Randall's parents were Robert Asa and Earl Bethenia "Teenie" Snell Randall. His father was from Pickens County, Alabama, and his mother was from Lowndes County, Mississippi. Robert and Earl Bethenia Randall had seven children. They were Vera Maude, John Thomas, James Asa, Robert McPheron, Brantley Harold, Freddie, Earl, Nettie, and Jesse Shull, my great-grandfather.

In the year 2000, I am able to trace kinship to Randalls who presently live in Pickens County, Alabama. Several church cemeteries in Pickens County, including the Providence Baptist Church, the Tabernacle Methodist Church, and the Pine Grove United Methodist Church, are the final resting places of many Randalls.

Jesse Shull Randall and Annie Johnson were married in Carroll County, Mississippi, on August 1, 1892. Jesse was 21 and Annie was 18.

Jesse and Annie had seven children. My grandmother, Willie Mae, was their oldest child. Mood was the second child. All of his nieces, nephews, grandnieces and grandnephews called him "Big Bud." Big Bud moved to New Orleans as a young man and married Louise Leonard, a registered nurse. We all called her "Aunt Lou." Big Bud and Aunt Lou lived on Maple Street in New Orleans. He worked for the Corps of Engineers. They had no children. After living in New Orleans many years, they moved to Vaiden and lived for a few years. Both in failing health, they returned to live in New Orleans and died within a few months of each other in the early 1960's. They are buried in the Greenwood Cemetery in New Orleans.

Jesse and Annie's next child was Jessie Ruth. She married James Pollard. They were both Carroll County natives and most likely lived in Carroll County all of their lives. Their children were Dennis, William, Mary Elizabeth "Kick," and Sarah Lynn. Other children of Jesse and Annie were John Haman, Annie Lloyd, Leonard, and Lynn. John Haman married Mary Lena Marshall and they had two children, Hilda Annette and Marvin "Buddy." Annie Lloyd "Nan," was married to Oscar Adolphus Simpson. For years they lived in Marks, Mississippi. Their children were Oscar Adolphus Simpson, Jr., Elizabeth Ann, Mae Rae, and Charles Randall. Leonard married, but I have no record of his wife's name. Lynn married John Ward Eades. Their two children were John Ward Eades, Jr., and Billy Randall Eades. All of my grandmother's siblings I knew well except John Haman, who died when I was a young child.

Jesse's children called him Papa, and his grandchildren and great-grandchildren called him Papa Randall. He is the only great-grandparent that I remember, and I have only fond memories of him.

My memory of him is that he lived with his daughter, Lynn Randall Eades, in Vaiden. I remember him as a tall skinny man with black hair with a small amount of gray sneaking into it. When I saw him, he always had a walking cane and seemed to always be chewing tobacco. He was always up and about and his mind was good.

He was a great teaser, using his walking cane to point toward you if he wanted you to listen to him. You would know by the tone of his voice if he were teasing or if the cane was his way of disciplining you. He always was neatly dressed in a pair of slacks and cotton shirt, never in blue jeans, overalls or any other type of work clothes.

## Other Folks Remember Him

On March 9, 2000, Louise Eades Noah, the wife of Jesse Randall's grandson, Kenneth Anderson Noah, told me the following when asked if she remembered Papa Randall. Her first response was: "Oh Lord yes, I remember him." She told about an occasion when Ken, her husband, and Ken's father, Tom, had gone into the town of Vaiden and a storm came up. When Ken and Tom returned from town, Papa Randall said to Ken, "Louise and yo mama carried that baby down into the ditch." Ken asked Papa Randall, "What did you do?" Papa Randall responded, "I went too God dask it." That baby was Ken and Louise's son, Kenneth Ray, my first cousin.

Papa Randall's granddaughter, Ruth, shared this memory of her grandfather with me on December 31, 2000. In her own words, "I begged and begged him for a chew of tobacco. One day Papa Randall and I were helping to fertilize some crop the family was growing. We were sitting on the back of a pick-up truck when I asked again for a chew of his tobacco. This time he gave it to me and told me not to tell my mama. After chewing the tobacco, I got sick. I wobbled to the house. Papa Randall had to tell Mama that I wanted the tobacco, and he gave it to me."

On April 18, 2002, a granddaughter, Bobbie Noah Smith, wrote this about Papa Randall. "I was dating Forrest Shelton, and one Sunday afternoon, Forrest and I were going for a ride. But Mama and Daddy wanted to go somewhere, and wouldn't leave me there alone with Forrest. Papa Randall was there, and he told them to go ahead and he would stay with me. So Mama and Daddy went and Papa Randall stayed. For years he teased me about how far I was sitting away from Forrest on his watch."

## He takes another wife

His first wife died on January 3, 1921, and sometime prior to 1922, Papa Randall married Mittie Mae McDaniel Randall, his brother Robert's widow. They had one child, Ouida. This wife was called Aunt Mittie by the family.

## End of Life

Papa Randall died on February 13, 1953, at the home of his daughter, Lynn Randall Eades, in Vaiden, Mississippi. His death certificate says that he died of uremia which was caused by nephrosclerosis and generalized arteriosclerosis. His death certificate says that his occupation was farming. My father, his oldest living grandchild, was 40 years old and I, his oldest great-grandchild, was 14 years old.

He was 84 years old when he died, a long life for his generation. At the time of his death, he had nineteen living grandchildren and sixteen great-grandchildren. He had seen the death of only one of his seven children.

During his lifetime there were 17 different presidents of the United States. He was born during the administration of Andrew Johnson, and his life ended during the Dwight Eisenhower presidency. After Andrew Johnson, those who served as United States Presidents were Ulysses Grant, Rutherford Hayes, James Garfield, Chester Arthur, Grover Cleveland, Benjamin Harrison, William McKinley, Theodore Roosevelt, Howard Taft, Woodrow Wilson, Warren Harding, Calvin Coolidge, Herbert Hoover, Franklin Delano Roosevelt, Harry Truman, and Dwight Eisenhower.

It is interesting to note that Andrew Johnson, Chester Arthur, and Theodore Roosevelt were elected vice presidents and became president when the president was assassinated. Both Abraham Lincoln and William McKinley were serving their second term, but James Garfield was in his first term for only six months when he was assassinated.

Harry Truman became president when Franklin Delano Roosevelt died in office in his fourth term. No other president had ever before served more than two terms. In 1951, the United States Congress passed a law to limit a president's serving more than two terms.

When he was born there were only 37 states. When he died there were forty-eight. Those territories that became states during his lifetime were Colorado, North Dakota, South Dakota, Montana, Washington, Idaho, Wyoming, Utah, Oklahoma, New Mexico, and Arizona. After 1912, when New Mexico and Arizona became states, there were not any new states added until Hawaii and Alaska became states in 1959.

Papa Randall was born shortly after the United States Civil War, and during his lifetime the United States engaged in the Spanish-American War when the United States took control of Puerto Rico and annexed Hawaii. He also lived through World War I, World War II, and the Korean Conflict.

Part 1B: Annie Johnson Randall, my father's maternal grandmother, was born on June 13, 1872 in Carroll County, Mississippi. Ulysses Grant was president of the United States.

Her parents, Gilbert and Emily Blakely Johnson, had seven children. They were James Monroe, Jesse, Martha, Cora, Dora, Elizabeth, and Annie, my great-grandmother.

Annie's father, Gilbert Johnson, was a Confederate soldier in the 29th Mississippi Infantry in the Civil War, and two of her great-grandfathers participated in the Revolutionary War. This is explained in Chapter 1.

## Other comments

My grandmother, Willie, on one occasion—and on only one that I remember—talked about her mother being a good housekeeper. My Aunt Ruby Annie Noah Jones, her granddaughter, was named for her. Otherwise, her personal history is lost. She is the only great—grandparent that I do not have a photograph of so can only imagine what she would have looked like.

## End of Life

Mama Randall was 48 years old when she died. According to her death certificate, she died on January 3, 1921, at home of chronic tuberculosis. Her death certificate records her occupation as home without any other details. My father, her oldest living grandchild, was six years old.

Both Jesse and Annie Johnson Randall are buried in the Old Salem Cemetery—originally the cemetery of the Old Salem Presbyterian Church, a church no longer in existence—in Carroll County, Mississippi, as are three of their seven children, Willie, John Haman and Leonard.

**Jesse Shull Randall**

## Part 2: Robert Dugan Noe and Sarah Ellen Sandlin Noe

Part 2 A: Robert Dugan Noe (Noah), my father's paternal grandfather was born on April 15, 1867, in Lamar County, Alabama. The year of his birth, Andrew Johnson, who succeeded Abraham Lincoln when he was assassinated, was president of the United States. There were 37 states in the Union. Nebraska had been admitted in March 1867, a month prior to his birth.

Research shows that his mother was Mary Agnes Tate Noe. According to Mary Noah Day—daughter of Luther Noah and a first cousin of my grandfather, Tom Noah—Robert's father's name was James. However, I have never been able to trace this line. Robert Dugan Noah had a brother, Luther, and a sister, Martha.

Robert Dugan Noe and Sarah Ellen Sandlin were married in Lamar County, Alabama, on August 27, 1885. A copy of their marriage certificate shows that the marriage took place in Lamar County, Alabama, at the home of Catherine Sandlin, who was Sarah's mother.

Thomas Anderson "Tom," was their oldest child. The other two children were Henry Melton and Ollie.

Tom is discussed in Chapter 3.

Henry Melton married Mary Johnston in Carroll County, Mississippi. They had eight children. They were Henry Melton, Jr., Marine, Thomas Anderson (same name exactly as his uncle and my grandfather), Curren, Pernella, Evelyn "Sissie," Bishop, L.V. "Bay," and Benjamin Washington, who was called "Preacher" and "Little Son." I have met all of these children of my great aunt and uncle, although I have known some of them better than others.

Ollie married Jesse Cleveland Noe in Alabama. Their children were Glaly, Ernestine, Christine, and Geraldine. At the time I wrote this book, I had the opportunity to meet only Geraldine. The rest of her siblings died before I was able to make contact. I was three years old when this great-grandfather of mine died, but I have no memory about him other than what was told to me. His children called him "Papa," and his two sons' grandchildren called him "Utta Papa." I also called him "Utta Papa."

## Family Leaves Alabama for Mississippi

In the winter of 1895, Robert Dugan Noe left Lamar County, Alabama, for Mississippi. Along with him were his mother, Mary; his brother, Luther; his sister, Martha, and her son George; and his two young boys, Tom and Henry. Tom, my grandfather, was nine years old and Henry was seven.

What follows is information told to me by Utta Papa's oldest grandchild, Henry Melton (H.M.) Noah, Jr. on August 6, 1988, at the Henry Noah, Sr. family reunion in Lake Village, Arkansas. H. M. remembered: "They were headed for the Mississippi Delta, but they never made it there. They arrived in Carroll County on Christmas Eve 1895 in a covered wagon. It was snowing and a Mr. Heggie who lived near Black Hawk, Mississippi, told them they could stay until the weather got better. In March the weather got better, and Mr. Heggie agreed that they could plant cotton. They stayed with Mr. Heggie two or three years."

Perhaps it was in the interest of pragmatism that Utta Papa took his boys to work in the cotton fields in the Mississippi Delta. But that is only a guess, and no living person knows why his three-year old daughter, Ollie, and his first wife, Sarah, were left behind in Alabama. It is not known whether Tom and Henry ever saw their mother again. My Aunt, Bobbie Noah Smith, has more than once said to me that she wished she had known this grandmother of hers when she was alive. Clearly Tom and Henry saw their sister, Ollie, again as the photograph of the three of them proves it so.

## He takes another wife

Robert Dugan Noah and Mattie Fisher were married on March 9, 1898 in Carroll County. We called this stepmother of my grandfather "Granny" and my grandfather called her "Mama." I knew and loved Granny and did think of her as my great-grandmother even though she wasn't. She seemed to love all of us, too.

Mattie and Robert Dugan Noah

Robert and Matte Fisher Noah had four girls, Alberta, Minnie, Mae and Mattie. I knew all of them, some better than others.

Alberta married Edward Kimes. Their children are Mamie, Edwin, Pauline, Eunice, Melvin, Alvin, Grace, and Rena. I have not known any of them well.

Minnie married Johnny B Lee. Their children are Robert E. "R. E.," John B "Junior," Ruben Odell "Dell," and Mary Elizabeth "Sissy." I have known each of them well.

Mae married John Boone. Their children are Sarah Mae, Margaret "Lovie," James William "Brother," Bernice, and Janice. I have known all of them, but some better than others.

Mattie married Charles Melton. They had no biological children but did adopt a young girl, Helen, whom I have always considered part of my extended family.

## He Moved on

After the two or three years on Mr. Heggie's place, Utta Papa moved to the Old Salem Community in Carroll County. Neither he nor any of the others in that party ever made it to the Mississippi Delta. Carroll County, where he spent the rest of his life, is in the hills. Of the original seven who left Alabama together, only Martha Noe Sandlin and her son George moved away.

The Mississippi Delta is known for its rich soil, but in the hills of Carroll County in the Old Salem Community, my great-grandfather prospered. From his accomplishments he seemed industrious, diligent, and hard-working. At one time during his life there he owned a grocery store, a cotton gin, and could do blacksmith work. He had a grist mill where people in the community brought their shelled corn to be ground into cornmeal. This grist mill was still in use in the late 1940s after his death, and I remember my father taking corn there to have it ground into meal.

## Name Change from Noe to Noah

Robert Dugan Noah, a great-grandfather of mine, is on the Lamar County, Alabama, 1870 census as R. D. with his mother listed as Mary Noe. On the 1880 Lamar County Census, R.D., his brother, Luther, and sister, Martha are listed with their mother, Mary Noe. The above grandson who gave me the information about their migration to Mississippi told me what he knew about the name change. He said that his grandfather bought groceries from Mr. Cade Armstrong in Vaiden, and that Mr. Armstrong was talking to his grandfather one day and told him that from that time on he would be a Noah and not a Noe.

This cannot be verified, but I did know Mr. Cade Armstrong. He was a member of Shongalo Presbyterian Church in Vaiden and I have read in a reference book that Noah was Hebrew for Noe.

Mr. Cade did not have a grocery store at the time that I knew him, but he owned a hardware store on what we called Front Street of Vaiden, and my grandfather, Tom, worked for him when he first moved to Vaiden in nineteen forty-nine.

## Other Folks Remember Him

In the early 1980s, I went to see Minnie Noah Lee, one of my grandfather's daughters by his second wife. She gave me the following account of her life at home in the Old Salem Community when she was growing up. This would have been in the time period of the 1920s and 1930s.

Minnie said they had to walk about one-fourth of a mile to the mailbox, and that she went to school in a wagon that was pulled by mules. According to Minnie, her family enjoyed many modern conveniences. They had a crank telephone and carbide lights.

Her father had an Overland car, and in March 2000 Minnie's son, Dell, gave me a photograph of this car with his grandfather and grandmother standing beside it. By Minnie's account, her father did not help in the kitchen, but all of the female children did field work. None of them used a plow, but they chopped and picked cotton.

Another account of Dell's regarded his grandfather's Overland car. In Dell's own words, "One day 'AnDaddy'—name his daughter's children called him—got ready to go into the town of Vaiden. He got dressed, sat down to put on his shoes and socks, and discovered he didn't have a pair of socks for some unknown reason. So he says to Granny "this is a hell of a note, a man driving an $1100 car and has no socks.'"

Bobbie Noah Smith remembered her grandfather on April 18, 2002. "I used to go to his house and watch them grind corn into meal every Saturday. We always went to his birthday party at his house. There were large crowds. Granny made the best big biscuits. I would spend the night with them. We would sit at the kitchen table, and she would leave the oven door open with the biscuits to keep them warm. I will always remember Marie Stuart came to tell Daddy about the death of his father riding on a horse. Daddy sat down and cried."

My father, Robert Randall Noah, remembered his grandfather in this way on November 25, 1994. "Utta Papa ground corn, plowed cotton and corn, and he sharpened tools."

**Robert Dugan and Mattie Fisher Noah
with Grandchildren on his 71st Birthday 1938**

## End of Life

Robert Dugan Noah died on April 16, 1942, in Carroll County, Mississippi. He was 75 years and one day old when he died, and for his generation he, also, lived a long life. His death certificate gives cardio-renal hypertension as the cause of his death. His second wife, Mattie Fisher Noah, died on May 28, 1966. She was 87 old and had outlived her husband by twenty-five years. I attended her funeral at the Blackmonton Presbyterian Church in Carroll County, Mississippi.

Both Robert Dugan and Mattie Fisher Noah are buried in the Old Salem Cemetery in Carroll County.

Part 2 B: Sarah Ellen Sandlin Noe, my father's paternal grandmother, was born on September 12, 1869. Ulysses Grant was President of the United States. Her parents were Anderson and Catherine Turman Sandlin, and she was their only child. According to her granddaughter, Geraldine Noe Floyd, her full name was Sarah Ellen Emaline Elvira Nancy Matilda Louisa Mary Jane Sandlin. Her mother was forty-five years old at the time of her birth and, realizing she would not have more children, named this one child for many family members.

She was born the same year as another great-grandparent of mine, Jesse Shull Randall. It is also interesting to note that they died within a year of each other, both in their eighties.

However, this great-grandmother was unknown to any of her sons' children or grandchildren. It was not until the late 1970s when I traveled to Sulligent, Alabama, in search of my roots, that our family found out that this great-grandmother did not die until 1952. I graduated from the eighth grade that same year. She is my only great-grandmother who outlived her husband.

Ollie's daughter, Geraldine Noe Floyd, is a grandchild who knew Sarah because Ollie was the only child of Robert and Sarah Sandlin Noe left behind in Alabama with her mother when the rest of the family migrated to Mississippi.

According to Geraldine, her grandmother never talked about her husband. Nor did she ever mention her two sons. It is a great mystery and will remain so, as there's neither oral nor written information available. If Sarah grieved for her sons who had moved with their father to Mississippi, it was not expressed.

In a telephone call on May 19, 2000, Geraldine told me that her grandmother always lived with Ollie after Ollie married. Geraldine said, "Grandmother did not work, but did help with home chores. She would shell peas, wash dishes, and do other little odd jobs." Geraldine said she would sit in her lap, and she reminisced about old times, and read the Bible to her grandchildren. According to Geraldine, her grandmother never went any place except to visit a cousin.

On February 16, 2002, this same granddaughter shared another bit of information. "It was told to me that Mama was three years old, she and her mother watched as the wagon pulled away with the rest of the family, not realizing they would never meet again."

## End of Life

Sarah Ellen Sandlin Noe died in 1952. Her oldest grandchild, Henry Melton Noah, Jr., the son of her second child, whom she never laid her eyes on, was 41 years old. My father, another grandchild, was 38 years old and I, one of her many great-grandchildren whom she never knew, was thirteen years old.

Sarah Ellen Sandlin Noe is buried beside her daughter, Ollie, in the Pine Springs Cemetery outside of Sulligent, Alabama.

**Sarah Ellen Sandlin Noe**

# Part 3: Allen and Narcissor Trotter Compton

Part 3 A: Allen Compton, my mother's paternal grandfather, was born on October 10, 1835, in Mississippi. He was the oldest of my great-grandparents. Andrew Jackson was president of the United States.

His parents were Drury and Jane Compton. I do not know if he had brothers and sisters. At the time of his birth, there were 24 states in the United States Union, Missouri having been admitted as the twenty-fourth.

My mother was a young girl when her grandfather died, but she did tell me that he was a tall, red-headed Irishman, and that he was from Old Middleton—originally part of Carroll County—in present day Montgomery County, Mississippi.

Allen Compton and Narcissor Elymria Trotter were married in Carroll County, Mississippi on November 06, 1857. They had nine children. A page from the family Bible documented by their grandchild and my aunt, Verna Mann Duke, lists some of their children and in my Family Tree Maker Program I have others. They were Elizabeth "Lizzie," Thomas Luther, Allen Ethelior "Thelia," Artimisa, James Rufus, Mary Frances, Minnie Clinton, William Drew, and Maggie Bell, my grandmother. I have a total of nine children listed. From this group of nine children, I knew two well, my grandmother Maggie and her sister Allen Ethelior. Her great-grand nieces and nephews called her "Cedy." I also knew of one other sibling of my grandmother, Maggie. Mother called her Aunt Molly, but I do not know which of the nine children she was. Aunt Molly married a Smith. Mother talked about at least two children of Aunt Molly. They were Edgar and Leila-pronounced lee-I-la.

## End of Life

Allen Compton was 87 years old when he died, and his life span was the longest of any of my great-grandparents. He died on February 10, 1923. Warren Harding was president of the United States. At the time of Allen's birth, there were 24 states in the Union and by his death there were forty-eight. His life span encompassed the Mexican-American War, the United States Civil War, in which he served in the Calvary F as a Confederate States of America soldier, the Spanish-American War, and World War I. He had seen 11 Southern states—South Carolina was the first and Mississippi was the second—withdraw from the Union, and after the United States Civil War he had seen those same states readmitted to the Union.

Part 3 B: Narcissor Elmyria Trotter Compton, my mother's maternal grandmother, was born on October 9, 1836, either in Mississippi or Tennessee. President Andrew Jackson was serving his second term as the President of the United States.

Her parents were Thomas and Mary Trotter. She was a twin to Artimissa Elvira Trotter.

## End of Life

Narcissor Trotter Compton died on September 6, 1906. Allen and Narcissor Trotter Compton are buried in the Enon Methodist Church Cemetery in Carroll County. Allen's tombstone is inscribed with the fact that he was a Confederate soldier. Narcissor's tombstone is inscribed with "mother and wife and children of A. G. Compton.

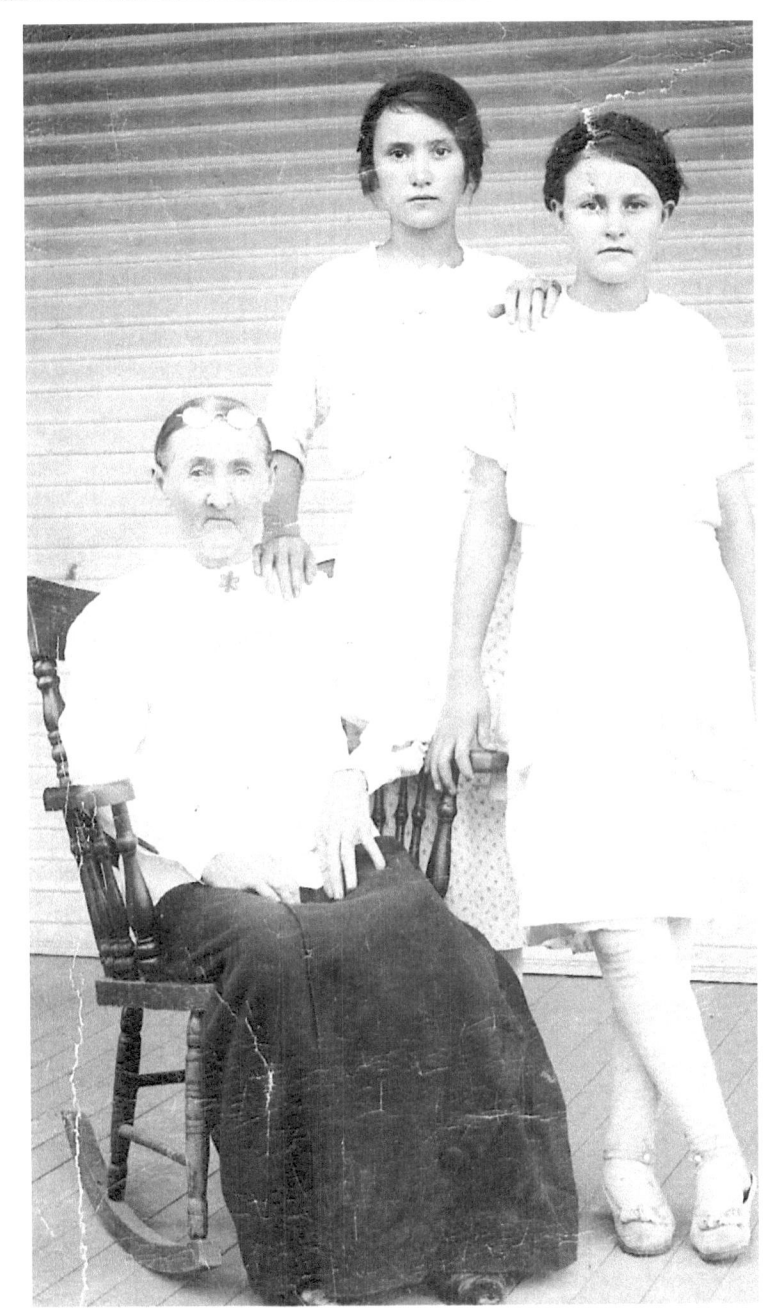

Seated: Artimissa "Missy" Trotter Turnipseed twin sister of
Narcissor Trotter Compton with two of her nieces Allen Ethelior
"Thelia" and Maggie Compton

**Allen and Narcissor Trotter Compton**

# Part 4: John Wishum and Sarah Collier Mann

Part 4 A: John Wishum Mann, my mother's paternal grandfather, was born in Mississippi on September 5, 1859, in either Clark or Carroll County, Mississippi. His parents were J.E. (German) and Elmyria Ringer Mann, and they were married in Clark County, Mississippi. J.E. (German) and Elmyria Ringer Mann had six children. They were John Wishum, Victoria, Narmie, Joseph, Withe, and J. E. (Jud).

When he was born James Buchanan, the fifteenth president of the United States, was in office. There were thirty-three states in the Union. Oregon was admitted as the thirty-third on February 14, 1859. He was one year old when the Southern states began to secede from the Union.

John Wishum Mann and Sarah Collier were married on January 18, 1877, in Carroll County, Mississippi. John was 18 and Sarah was about the same age.

Sarah and John Mann had 8 children, all boys. They were Walter, Floyd Fletcher, Verge, Herman, Charles, Grenade, Turner, and Ledell, who was known as Dell. Floyd was my grandfather.

I am able to document only the information that I have in my Family Tree Maker. Verge and his wife had four children: Virgil, Bernice, Willie Mae, and Ruth. Grenade married Lena Johnson, and they had one child, Earl. Dell married Juanita Andrews, and they had three children, Sarah Dell, Bonnie Jean and Y. Gillespie—a son who died young. Turner married Lola Carpenter. Their children were Herman, Faye, Margaret, Mary Frances, Ray and John Alton.

This great-grandfather of mine left a legacy. It was not unusual for my mother to talk about her grandfather, whom she called Grandpa Mann. He was a farmer and a carpenter, and it is his carpentry that I have knowledge about. He is given credit for building the pulpit at the Enon Methodist Church. He also built furniture: armoires, kitchen cabinets, cedar chests, and china cabinets.

He is in a photo in the Enon Singing School in 1911. Three of his sons Floyd, Dell and Turner sang in the choir at Enon, also.

Gionne Graetz, great-great-granddaughter of John Wishum Mann standing in front of a china cabinet that he built. Photo made of her Mother's Day 2004 in Alexandria, Virginia

Enon Methodist Church Singing School 1911 second man on the left
John Wishum Mann *Note organ on the outside of the church.

**John Wishum and Sarah Collier Mann**

Enon Methodist Church Pulpit built by John Wishum Mann
In photo are five of his grandchildren
From left to right: Sarah Dell Mann Bell, Mary Frances Mann Shelton,
Earl Mann, Margaret Mann Griffin, and Bonnie Mann Simpson.

## Other Folks Remember Him

On April 21, 2002, his granddaughter, Sarah Dell Mann Bell, remembered her grandfather while we were sitting on her front porch, a place where she and her grandfather sat. "When I was a small child, I would sit on the front porch with Grandpa Mann, and he would tell about his early childhood in or near Artesia, Mississippi." She also said in each son's family Grandpa Mann had a favorite child. "I was his favorite child in my daddy's family, and in Uncle Floyd's family, Verna was his favorite child."

## End of Life

John Wishum Mann was 74 years old when he died, another long life for a man of his generation, outliving his wife by 15years. He died on July 23, 1934, in Carrollton, Mississippi, at the home of his son, Dell, with whom he had lived. His death certificate says that he died of arteriosclerosis, and Dell's children, Sarah Dell and Bonnie Jean, told me that Grandpa Mann had lost his mind, and would wander off from home. In their own words, "Daddy would have to go looking for him and he would be walking toward Enon, the place he had lived most of his life."

Part 4 B: Sarah Collier Mann was born in 1858 in Mississippi. The United States President was James Buchanan. Sarah's parents were John and Abigail Tisdale Collier. I have listed in my Family Tree Maker four children. They were Richard Watson, Walter, Mary, and Sarah, my great-grandmother. I have no recall of anyone talking about this great-grandmother of mine.

## End of Life

Sarah Collier Mann died on July 4, 1919, at the age of sixty or sixty-one, a second great-grandmother who died at a young age.

John Wishum and Sarah Collier Mann are buried in the Enon Methodist Church Cemetery in Carroll County, Mississippi.

**Dell and Verge Mann**

**Turner Mann**

# Chronology

| | |
|---|---|
| 1835 | Allen G. Compton was born in Carroll County, Mississippi, on October 10, 1835. He was born the same year as Samuel Langhorne Clemens who took the pseudonym of Mark Twain. |
| 1836 | Narcissor Elmyria Trotter was born on October 09, 1836 either in Mississippi or Tennessee. Eighteen thirty-six was the year of the Texas Revolution in which the settlers of Texas, mostly from the United States, declared their independence from Mexico. After these Texas settlers declared their independence, the Mexican army arrived to put down the rebellion. That army captured the Alamo, killing all 187 Texans including Davy Crockett and Jim Bowie. However, that victory lasted only a short time in that one month later, Santa Ana, the Mexican commander was captured and forced to surrender Texas at the Battle of San Jacinto. |
| 1857 | Allen Compton and Narcissor Elmyria Trotter were married in Carroll County, Mississippi on November 6, 1857. |
| 1857 | Same year of the marriage of Allen and Narcissor, Mardi Gras's first carnival society, the Mystic Krewe of Comus, began planning and paying for parades in New Orleans, Louisiana. |
| 1858 | Sarah Collier was born in Carroll County, Mississippi. The year of her birth Abraham Lincoln made strong antislavery speech in Springfield, Illinois. |
| 1859 | John Wishum Mann was born on September 5, 1859, in Clark or Carroll County, Mississippi. |
| 1859 | That same year that Charles Darwin, the English naturalist established the theory of organic evolution known as Darwinism. On August 27, 1859, another world changing event took place; the first successful oil well was drilled in Pennsylvania. |
| 1861-1865 | United States Civil War was fought. |
| 1863 | Abraham Lincoln gave Gettysburg Address on November 19.1863, in Gettysburg, Pennsylvania. I memorized this in the fifth grade at Blackmonton School in 1949 approximately eighty-four years after it was given. |

1865 John Wilkes Booth shot President Abraham Lincoln while he and his wife, Mary Todd Lincoln, were sitting in the Ford Theatre in Washington, D.C. on April 14, 1865. He died the next day. He saw the end of the Civil War but was assassinated prior to the Southern states readmission to the union. Robert E. Lee had surrendered at Appomattox, Virginia, only five days before the assassination.

1866 Alfred Nobel invented dynamite.

1867 Robert Dugan Noe was born on April 15, 1867, in Lamar County, Alabama. The year of his birth the United States purchased the Alaska Territory from Russia for $7,200,000.

1869 Jesse Shull Randall was born on January 22, 1869, in Lowndes County, Mississippi. It was a year of transportation successes. The United States Transcontinental Railroad was completed at Promontory Point, Utah, and the Suez Canal, which linked the Mediterranean and the Red Sea was opened for business in Egypt.

1869 Sarah Ellen Sandlin was born on September 12, 1869, in Alabama.

1872 Annie Johnson was born in Carroll County, Mississippi on June 13, 1872.

1875 First Kentucky Derby held first Saturday in May in Louisville, Kentucky at Churchill Downs.

1877 John Wishum Mann and Sarah Collier were married on January 18, 1877, in Carroll County, Mississippi. The year of their marriage Thomas Edison filed a patent for the phonograph, and Alexander Graham Bell patented the telephone

1885 Robert Dugan Noe (later Noah) and Sarah Ellen Sandlin were married in Lamar County, Alabama on August 27, 1885. The year of their marriage the Washington Monument was completed in Washington D.C. In this year in Chicago, Illinois the world's first skyscraper as built.

1892 Jesse Shull Randall and Annie Johnson were married on August 01, 1892, in Carroll County, Mississippi. The year of their marriage, Ellis Island was opened New York, and the first of twelve million immigrants passed through its "golden door."

# Chapter 3   Grandparents and Great Aunt Allen Ethelior "Cedy"

Grandparents
Carolyn heeding
muted voices

I am a fortunate person in that I knew all of my grandparents and my great Aunt Thelia. Thelia, my grandmother Maggie's sister, seemed like a third grandmother. They were all born in the nineteenth century and all lived long enough to see all of their grandchildren.

Though my maternal grandparents lived with us in their old age for two to three years prior to my leaving Carroll County, Mississippi, I have more memories of my paternal grandparents. An easy explanation is that we lived much closer to my paternal grandparents during the first 15 years of my life.

## Part 1: Thomas Anderson and Willie Mae Randall Noah

Part 1 A: Thomas Anderson Noah, my paternal grandfather, was born in Lamar County, Alabama, on June 25, 1886. His parents were Robert Dugan and Sarah Ellen Sandlin Noe. He is my only grandparent who was not a native of Carroll County, Mississippi. At the time of his birth, Grover Cleveland, the twenty-second president of the United States, was in office.

When he was nine years old, his father and many other family members left Alabama for Mississippi. Details are under my great—grandfather, Robert Dugan Noah. He was only nine years old and without his mother for the rest of his life. If he missed her or grieved for her is unknown for he never did say. In fact my grandfather never showed grief. He and my grandmother buried four of their eight children. I knew him well and spent plenty of time with him, but I never saw him cry, nor did I ever hear him whisper a word about sadness. I wonder if that is the best way.

Thomas Anderson Noah married Willie Mae Randall on December 13, 1911, in Carroll County, Mississippi. He was twenty-five years old, although the marriage certificate says 21but this does not fit with his birthday, and she was eighteen. They were married over fifty years.

Tom and Willie had eight children. They were William Cade, Robert Randall, Mary Ellen, Kenneth Anderson, Tom Haman, Ruby Annie, Obie Louise, and Ruth. Several of the children had nicknames, Robert Randall; my father was called "Bubber" by his sisters and brother. Mary Ellen was called the endearing name of "City" by her siblings.

Only her father called Obie Louise by her first name. All others called her "Bob," nickname given to her—according to Bobbie herself—by Gladys Bacon, a neighbor and friend, who one day told her she looked so much like her grandfather, Robert Dugan Noah, that she was going to call her "Bob" from that day forward. The rest of the world followed suit. Today her friends call her "Bobbie," but family and folks who have known her forever call her Bob. The youngest child was called "Baby Ruth" by her family and friends for years. Other folks, including her husband, call her Ruth. However, because habits are hard to break, most of our family members continue to call her Baby Ruth.

Mary Ellen died on March 28, 1937, three months prior to the marriage of my parents. She died on Easter Sunday. Her sister, Bobbie, wrote this account of her sickness and death on April 18, 2002. "There was a bad storm, and City and Ken had walked to Utta Papa's. The next morning she complained of a sore throat to Daddy, and since she was going to school in Vaiden, Daddy told her to go to the doctor at lunch. She never came home. She stayed in town with Aunt Ruth for ten days to two weeks, getting worse all the time.

"She finally was taken to Grenada Hospital. I don't remember how long she lived, but Bubber was staying with her most of the time. She had to have blood transfusions. As well as I remember, he gave the blood. Bubber and Lynn—Mary Ellen's mother's sister—were with her when she died. After she died, Bubber came home and went to bed in the side room. I went into the room and Mama was sitting on the side of the bed. She told Bubber that the neighbors were making Ruth and me dresses to wear to the funeral. Bubber said, 'I would like for them to wear the red dresses you made.' Mama said, 'Son you don't wear red to a funeral.' We wore little brown pleated skirts.

"City died about 2:00 in the morning and was buried on that same day. That funeral was attended by one of the largest crowds I have ever seen in so short of time. Daddy never shed a tear. He couldn't. He would go off and sit by himself, and Mama cried every time her name was called. We soon learned not to talk about her. She had planned to go the nursing school in Jackson. That's enough sadness."

My father, Robert, had not only lost a sister, but he also lost a good friend, if not his best friend. I continue to shed tears when I hear this sad story.

Ken married Louise Eades, and they had two sons, Kenneth Ray and a second son who did not survive childbirth. Ruby married Marion McClellan "Sonny" Jones, and they had three children, Linda, Joe Don, and Marion. Bobbie married Rowland Smith, and they had two sons, Sidney and Michael "Mike." Ruth married Roy Eddins and they had one son, Donald "Don."

Tom was called "Daddy" by his children and his grandchildren called him "Daddy Tom." He wasn't an educated person, but he could read, write and do math. During his lifetime he did many types of work. Early in life he made living cotton farming and selling milk from his cows. He also drove a school bus, a pick-up truck with a wood enclosed cover over the back. After the move from Blackmonton to Vaiden, Daddy Tom worked in the hardware store of Mr. Cade Armstrong, and when he was in his late seventies he did custodial work at the Vaiden Courthouse.

My memories about him are many, fond, and indelible. He was always neatly dressed—my grandmother ironed his clothes that he wore every day—in those starched, creased, khaki pants and long—sleeved khaki shirts.

Another memory that sticks in my mind is that he took me to church in the Old Salem Presbyterian Church, and I was all dressed up in this thin organdy dress. I must have been between four and five years old.

When he was older, he regularly attended church at the Shongalo Presbyterian Church in Vaiden. He sat near the back row. But he had the habit of sniffling his nose, and you could hear him throughout the church, I thought.

Daddy Tom liked politics and delved into politics himself. On at least one occasion he ran for the Board of Supervisors in Carroll County and lost. He was elected to the Board of Aldermen and at the age of 74 he was serving a second term on that board.

## Others Remember Him

On November 25, 1994, his son, my father, remembered the following about his father. "He made molasses using both Louisiana and sorghum cane. He would put the cane in the mill and this squeezed the juice into a pan over a fire. The juice was then cooked in a long pan. When it was ready you opened the trough to let it drain into a big can. Later, small cans were filled from the larger can."

On August 24, 1995, Ruby Jones, Tom's daughter and my aunt, shared this memory of her father with me. She remembered Native American Indians camping on her father's land at Blackmonton and that he would give the Indians willow limbs for making baskets.

In a follow up of that memory, by telephone on May 24, 2002, when I asked Ruby for more information about the interaction with the Indians she said, "the Indians would not only make baskets, but made tables out of the willow limbs, and on the front of those little tables they placed a heart-shaped decoration made out of the willow limbs."

During that same telephone conversation, Ruby recalled a good deed of her dad's. "Sam and Esther Lee and their family were living in the Mississippi Delta and it flooded. Daddy went and rescued them out of the high water, brought them to live in the little house across the hollow from us. The Lee's lost everything they had in the flood. We took mattresses from our beds and gave to them."

Bobbie Smith, another daughter, wrote anecdotes about her father on April 18, 2002. "I never chopped much cotton, but I have put out fertilizer with a teaspoon by each stalk of corn. I remember one day Ruby and I were thinning corn. Daddy wanted it three feet apart. Well I thought I was doing a good job. I didn't thin one stalk because if I had it would have been more than three feet. Daddy was walking behind us, came to that spot, reached down, jerked that stalk of corn out of the ground and said, 'any damn fool knows that is not three feet apart. I looked at him and said 'any damn fool knows that is more than three feet apart.' I figured he would get mad, but he laughed and walked off."

Other written memories of Bobbie's: "Daddy was a good daddy, strict, oh yes. I can't remember him whipping me but two or three times, but that's all it took. He could look at me and that was punishment enough.

"Daddy was absolutely lost after Mama died. He didn't know how to boil water. But he wanted to stay at his home. I went home one weekend, and he was sitting on the front porch waiting for me. I said, 'Daddy, have you eaten supper?' He said, 'Yes, I ate some sardines.' That's where I lost it and I thought what are we doing?

"He would come to Jackson to stay with me, but he was miserable when he came. He had nothing to do. I would take him to the grocery store and it would take me three times as long with him strolling behind me. One day I asked Daddy if he would like to sit in the car. He said, 'I believe I will.' I went into the store and bought the groceries, and when I came out, Daddy said, 'I don't know why everyone doesn't get killed with people driving like mad.'

"Eventually he did go to Ruby's and Sonny's to stay, and it was Ruby who took him to the hospital, where he died."

On December 31, 2000, Ruth said, "Daddy was lazy and he liked me to watch him work." She gave this example. "He sharpened plow points by placing the points in hot coals, and he wanted me to stand by him while he was doing the job."

Ruth was not the only family member who said the same about him. I do not remember the laziness, but I did think that my grandmother pampered him. He would walk home for lunch every day, and in the winter time when he was ready to return to work, my grandmother would get his coat and help him put it on. She milked the cows, and did all of the cooking and housework.

Another memory of Ruth's on that same date involved her husband, Roy, and her son, Don. "Roy bought our first riding lawn mower, and he and Don had a little trailer they attached to the mower. Daddy got him a chair and placed it in the trailer. I can just see them now, with Don driving the riding lawn mower and Daddy sitting in the chair on the trailer riding around town."

Tom and Henry Noah with their Sister Ollie in Alabama around 1950

On March 9, 2000 Louise Eades Noah, his daughter-in-law, gave me some of the information that she remembered about Daddy Tom. In all seriousness she said, "I want to tell you something now—Daddy Tom was lazy." But she added that he was a good fellow. "I might not have graduated from high school if it had not been for him. I had to milk cows before going to school. This made me late for the school bus that Daddy Tom was driving, but he would wait on me."

Dell Lee, Daddy Tom's nephew, told me on March 12, 2000, that he remembered going to the Black Hawk Methodist Church with Uncle Tom to hear orphans from Jackson sing. He had no recall of why he was the only one going along. In another memory Dell said, "Uncle Tom was going to take me into the town of Vaiden, and Mama, Tom's sister, Minnie Noah Lee, told me I had to take a bath if I was going to town." Dell remembered, "I told Mama if I had to take a bath I am not going, but Mama told me I had to take a bath anyway. So I took my bath and got to go to town."

On March 11, 2000, my brother and his grandson, Billy Noah, remembered that Daddy Tom always wore khaki clothes, and that Daddy Tom would bring it to Billy's attention that he had bowlegs.

On April 19, 2002, another grandson, my brother, Bobby Noah remembered our paternal grandparents in this way. "I thought they were good grandparents. I was staying with them and Daddy Tom had a courthouse janitorial job. He got sick and I took over his courthouse job while he was sick. Mama City gave me lunch money."

## End of Life

Daddy Tom died on August 4, 1974. At the ripe old age of 88, he was taken by his daughter, Ruby Noah Jones, to the Tyler-Holmes Hospital in Winona, Mississippi, stayed a few days and died. His daughter, Ruth, was with him. His mind was good for his age, his heart gave out. The death certificate says he died of a coronary occlusion.

At the time of his birth in 1886 there were 38 states in the Union and at the time of his death there were fifty. During his lifetime there were 15 different presidents. Richard Milhaus Nixon was president at the time of his death, but within five days we were to have another president. Gerald Ford became president after Nixon was forced to resign or face impeachment due to the Watergate break-in.

He had lived through five wars in which the United States was involved; the Spanish-American, World War I, World War II, the Korean War, Vietnam Conflict and a large portion of the Cold War.

Part 1B: Willie Mae Randall Noah, my paternal grandmother, was born on June 5, 1893, in the Old Salem Community of Carroll County, Mississippi. She was the oldest child of her parents, Jesse Shull and Annie Johnson Randall, and the grandmother that I knew best.

Grover Cleveland was president of the United States when she was born, the same president who was in office when my grandfather was born. It is interesting to note, however, that Grover Cleveland is the only president elected to a second term that was not consecutive in that Benjamin Harrison was elected to the United States presidency in between Cleveland's first and second terms.

I was the oldest grandchild and I called my grandmother Mama, just as her children did. The rest of her grandchildren called her "Mama City," and sometimes it sounded like they were saying "Mama Thity."

She was a dominant figure in my life. To me Mama was a wonderful grandmother, and she treated me well. She was a loving but a tough lady. I learned a lot from her. Unfortunately, I didn't learn some of her best abilities, cooking and sewing.

Mama and I would have long talks mostly dealing with her feelings and worries about my family. But she expected a lot out of me, I tried to please her, and I worked hard to win her respect and admiration. I would help clean her house and do other little chores. I also liked the quiet time that I spent at my grandparents' home.

Many of my memories of my grandmother have to do with how hard she worked. She milked cows and sold milk and the butter she churned from the milk. After my grandparents moved into the town of Vaiden, they had only one cow, and my grandmother would go out into the cold winter weather to milk the cow while my grandfather remained in the warm house.

She was fussy about her sewing, too. I remember her complaining about people who sewed and left their knots untied. For herself, she would only make shirt waist dresses, and never would have had a Peter Pan collar. The last dress that she made for me in 1960 was a shirt waist dress.

Mama was especially particular about her washing and ironing. It was important to her that the clothes were whiter than white, and that you ironed white shirts, starched stiff, without leaving a wrinkle.

49

My other memories of her have to do with her willingness to take care of us when we were ill. My sister and I had a horrible case of the red measles, we had high fever, and our eyes hurt to the point that we had to have the room dark. As soon as the diagnosis was made, we went to my grandparents' to be cared for by my grandmother. We were there for a week. It is likely that we would have lived anyway, but it certainly helped my mother to know that her ill children were being cared for. Mother had two other small children to care for at that time.

Other good memories that stand out for me have to do with family holiday events. Mama cooked more food than I can account for, including chicken and cornbread dressing, ambrosia, mashed potatoes and gravy made with the chicken drippings, sweet potato casserole, corn, beans, English peas, ice box rolls, pecan pies, caramel cake, and fruit cake.

Mama could make a meal out of nothing. I especially remember her yeast rolls—we called them ice box rolls—corn bread, ice cream and caramel frosted cakes, the cake and frosting made from scratch. She never used a recipe book, but two recipes like hers follow. All were good, but the homemade ice cream and caramel cake frosting were scrumptious.

Mama made homemade ice cream often. When she expected a large crowd, a hand turned ice cream freezer was used, but often she placed the custard into the refrigerator freezer tray for freezing. It was delicious.

Here I will share a couple of recipes like hers:

## Ice box or yeast rolls

Heat 1 pint milk, 1cup water, 1 cup shortening, and 2 cups sugar to boiling, stirring constantly. Let cool. Add 1 package of yeast and all purpose flour to make consistency of cake batter. Let rise until twice in bulk. Add 1teaspoon salt, 1 teaspoon baking powder, a pinch of soda, and flour to make stiff dough. Roll out and place in a 350 degree oven for about twenty minutes.

Mama would make a batch of the rolls, serve them with butter—yes real butter—that she had churned from milk from the cow in her back yard. We added a little jelly to the rolls, and that was the entire meal.

## Caramel cake frosting

Here is a similar recipe to hers which I obtained from her daughter, Ruby Noah Jones, and her granddaughter, Linda Jones Darby, Ruby's daughter and Mama's granddaughter. 1 stick margarine, and 1 cup whipping cream. Cook on top of the stove until it is mixed together. Brown 2 cups granulated white sugar in a black skillet. Pour this mixture into the pan with the first mixture. Bring to a boil until it forms a soft ball in cold water. Beat with hand mixer. Apply to top of sheet cake or layered cake.

The above were her strengths, but she was not perfect. She was a terrible housekeeper, and when she washed dishes, she never quite finished the job. The kitchen counters were often left with odds and ends, plates, glasses, or other items that had food on them. It looked like she just got tired and quit.

She was a smoker. Her brothers and sisters were smokers, and at one time all of her children were smokers. Sometimes she would send me to buy Country Gentleman tobacco, which she used to roll her own cigarettes to smoke. She never in her life smoked in front of my grandfather, although they were married over 50 years. She would hear my grandfather come in a door, and on automatic she would put her cigarette out between her middle and first finger. Those fingers were stained brown. If my grandfather knew that she smoked, he never said one way or the other.

I often think of my grandmother when I hear of a child dying before the parent. My grandmother and grandfather buried four children. Their first son was three years old when he died according to dates printed on his tombstone in the Old Salem Cemetery. Another son died with pneumonia when he was fourteen months. A daughter died at the age of eighteen.

Yet another child, Ken, died at the age of forty-two. Louise Eades Noah, Ken's wife, gave this account of his death on December 27, 2002, at her home in Vaiden, Mississippi. My brother, Bobby, was living with Ken and Louise at the time. "Kenneth Ray, Bobby, and I went up to my sister Bell's [Bell was Louise's sister] to watch television. When we arrived back home, Ken was complaining of chest pain. I went to get Bob to go with me to take Ken to the Winona Hospital. When we got there the hospital didn't have any oxygen. Buddy Eades and I went to Greenwood and got an oxygen tent. He lived about a week until all of his organs shut down." Ken died on April 11, 1961. He is buried in the Old Salem Cemetery.

All those deaths must have shattered the lives of my grandparents, but neither of them ever talked about their feelings.

## Other Folks Remember Her

On December 31, 2000, her daughter Ruth remembered that her mother made all of her clothes until she was fifteen or sixteen years of age.

On March 9, 2000, when I first asked Louise Eades Noah, my grandmother's daughter-in-law, what she remembered about my grandmother, she said there was so much that it would be hard to condense it. Her first sentence was, "Mama Thity and I were so close." Louise also remembered that she was hard working and saved every penny.

Louise told a story that on one occasion Curren Noah, my grandfather's nephew, Louise, and my grandmother had been at the barn milking cows. On the way back to the house, my grandmother fell down with a bucket full of milk in each hand. Curren turned to Louise and said, "I bet she didn't spill a drop." Louise remembered, "We had to set our buckets down, get over being tickled, and help her to get up. Mind you, she had not spilled a drop." As Louise told this story to me, we both got tickled once again.

My brother, Billy, told me on March 11, 2000, that he liked the way she cooked and that Mama could "squeeze a nickel." On May 17, 2002, he recalled. "Mother [that's Billy's and my mother] said when she got married that she didn't know how to cook because her Aunt Thelia had done all of the cooking for her family and that Mama City taught Mother how to cook."

My brother Marvin, another grandson, recalled memories of my grandmother on July 5, 2002, "Mama City liked to play pranks. She and I were big buddies. One day she told me not to call Daddy Tom to eat." Mama City said, 'when dinner is ready, he'll be in here.'"

Dell Lee, my dad's first cousin, remembered this about my grandmother on March 12, 2000. Dell said. "I was sitting in the kitchen talking with my grandmother, [who was Mattie Fisher Noah] and Aunt Willie, when my brother Junior came into the kitchen. Aunt Willie says, 'Look yonder at that boy, he walks just like his grandfather [She was talking about Robert Dugan Noah], and as long as Junior lives, Mr. Noah will be here.'"

Mama's first cousin, Roscoe Johnson, told me on May 25, 1995, that he remembered my grandmother for her good cooking, hard work, and remembering everyone's birthday.

Her daughter, Bobbie, remembered her mother on April 18, 2002. "My mama tried to please everyone, and I know she was the best cook that there ever was. I have tried to make chicken dressing and cook green beans like hers. I just can't make the beans shrivel like she did, but of course she cooked them all morning. Everything that she cooked was good. She loved to go to the garden and pick her beans and can them.

"I remember when I was a little girl, we lived out in the country, and Lynn [Lynn was Mama's sister] would come out when the garden got ready. She and Mama canned the beans using a pressure cooker. One year, instead of using jars, they used cans like you buy in a grocery store. I can't remember how they sealed them, but after the pressure went down and they opened the pressure cooker, a can blew up. It got all over the place. We even pulled green beans out of Lynn's ears. It didn't scare them at all, but it made me afraid of a pressure cooker."

Bobbie had other memories. "When Daddy and Mama finally moved into the town of Vaiden, I was so proud. She had to bring her cow to milk, and she did that for years. Though her arthritis was taking its toll, she hobbled to the garden to gather fresh vegetables."

Bobbie was helpful and wrote one last memory. "After Ruby and Sonny bought the cotton gin, she cooked for them every day during ginning season. Sonny thought she was such a good cook. The day she went to the hospital the last time, she wanted to walk through the house. I will always say she had a premonition that it would be her last time to see her home. She never came back home."

On May 5, 2002 Charles "Chuck" Planer, Mama's grandson-in-law, remembered her for her cooking and said, "She reminded me of my own grandmother."

## End of Life

Lyndon Baines Johnson was president of the United States when Mama died on July 12, 1966, in the Tyler-Holmes Hospital in Winona, Mississippi. She was 73 years old. Her mind was good but her heart gave out. Her death certificate says she died of a myocardial infarction. The day she died I had driven from Montgomery, Alabama, to see her, but upon arrival I was told that she had died. Her daughter, Ruth, was in the hospital room with her.

Tom and Willie Mae Randall Noah are buried in the Old Salem Cemetery in Carroll County, Mississippi.

**Willie and Tom Noah with Five of Their Children**
**Ruth, Ruby, Ken, Bobbie, and Robert**

**Willie and Tom Noah Christmas 1965**

Tom and Willie Mae Randall Noah
50th Wedding Anniversary 1961

**Four Generations: Robert Noah, Carolyn Noah Graetz.
Tom Noah with Great-grandson Derek Graetz**

**Derek Graetz, Tom Noah, Robert Noah, and Gionne Graetz**

## 2: Floyd Fletcher Mann and Maggie Bell Compton Mann and her sister, Allen Ethelior "Cedy" Compton

Part 2 A: Floyd Fletcher Mann, my maternal grandfather, was born in Carroll County, Mississippi, on July 29, 1880. His parents were John Wishum and Sarah Collier Mann. Rutherford Hayes from Fremont, Ohio, was serving as the nineteenth president of the United States.

Floyd Fletcher Mann and Maggie Bell Compton were married either in 1900 or 1901 in Carroll County, Mississippi. They had four children: They were Percy Clyde, Verna Lorena, Victor Harmon, and my mother, Susie Evelyn "Dollie".

Percy left Mississippi in the 1940s and moved to Great Falls, Montana. He lived there for years and wrote home about sheep shearing in Montana and how horribly cold it was in the winter. He never saw his parents again. Percy later moved to Ogden, Utah. I visited him there in 1967. In 1980, my brother Bobby went to Utah and brought him to Mississippi for a visit. When Percy died my sister, Sarah, and her husband had his body shipped back to Mississippi so he could be buried beside his parents in the Enon Methodist Cemetery.

Verna married William Duke. They had one child, Janice Noel. Victor married Vera Wilshire. They had six children: Martha Louise, Dorothy Jean, Virginia Ruth, William Harmon "Bubber," Bobby Ann, and Victor Hayden. Everyone called them Martha, Dorothy, Ginger, Bubber, Bobbie Ann and Hayden.

Floyd's children called him Papa, and his grandchildren called him Papa Mann.

I do have some fond memories of him. When we were children and we would go to visit my grandparents, he would play games with us. We would sit on his lap and there was this little game that he would play. I remember only "William ah William ah Trimble Toe" was part of what he said using our fingers to say this little verse. Another little verse in which he used our fingers again was "this little piggie went to the market, this little piggie stayed home" and when he arrived at the little finger he would say "and this little piggie fell down and cried all the way home and now smell of your hand." I guess the little piggie must have spilled something that did not smell good.

**Floyd and Maggie Compton Mann**

Floyd and Maggie Compton Mann and their Children
left to right: Victor, Percy, Dollie in Maggie's lap, and Verna

Maggie Mann with four
Grandchildren
left to right: Virginia
Mann, Carolyn Sue
Noah, Hayden Mann,
and Bobbie Ann Mann

## Other Folks Remember Him

On March 11, 2000, my brother Billy remembered that he could stop blood on animals. On April 21, 2002, his niece, Sarah Dell Mann Bell, confirmed what Billy had remembered about Papa Mann. Sarah Dell said, "People from all over the area depended on Uncle Floyd for this service."

On that same day Sarah Dell said, "We loved to go to Uncle Floyd's and Aunt Maggie's. One afternoon we planned to go to Uncle Floyd's and it rained. So my parents decided not to go. But Bonnie [Sarah's sister] and I cried. We did end up going and, sure enough, we got stuck. We had to get out and walk the rest of the way and it was late at night when we got there."

On March 14, 2000, his niece, Margaret Mann Griffin, remembered him in this way. "He and his brothers, Dell and Turner, my daddy, liked to sing. I never saw them sit any place in the Enon Methodist Church other than in the choir."

On January 26, 2001, my sister Sarah remembered Papa Mann in this way. "I was spending the week with them during the Enon Revival Week, and we walked through the woods to see Lula Mae Carpenter. On the way back home we picked sweet gum from the sweet gum trees to chew." Lula Mae was a well-known member of the Enon Methodist Church and a good friend of my grandparents and my mother.

By telephone conversation on May 5, 2002, Mother's high school friend, Agnes McGregor McArthur, remembered that my grandfather had a job working on the roads in the Enon area of Carroll County.

## End of Life

On September 24, 1957, I wrote in my diary that I had a letter from Mother. She wrote that Papa Mann was going to the Old Men's Home. I cried. He was being placed in Whitfield [Whitfield was an institution for the insane, and in the case of my grandfather, he had senile dementia.] where he remained for the rest of his life. He died there on August 26, 1961. President John F. Kennedy, the thirty-fifth president of the United States, was in office. At the time of Papa Mann's birth in 1880, there were 38 states. When he died there were 50 states. He had lived through many wars in which the United States was involved: the Spanish-American

War, World War I, World War II, the Korean War, and the Cold War's beginning, but not its end.

Part 2 B: Maggie Bell Compton Mann, my maternal grandmother, was born in Carroll County, Mississippi, on February 14, 1879. Her parents were Allen and Narcissor Trotter Compton. Like her husband she was born during the presidential administration of Rutherford Hayes.

Her children called her Mama, and her grandchildren called her Mama Mann. I remember her well, but I have little recall of anything that she did. She always seemed old and feeble to me. I have no recall of any type of housework, gardening, or cooking that she did.

I do remember that she grew flowers in pots and in discarded old dishpans. It was through her that I became acquainted with summer blooming flowers including four o' clocks, zinnias, geraniums, and marigolds.

In the last few years of her life, she lived with our family, and the only thing that I remember about her is that she was bedridden and sat on the side of the bed with her feet hanging off to the side night and day. Her feet were very swollen, and she never put on shoes or slippers.

## Others Folks Remember Her

My brother, Billy, recalled in March 2000, "Daddy really liked her and I think it was because she liked to drink whiskey."

On January 26, 2001, my sister, Sarah Lou Noah Planer, remembered our grandmother in this way. "Mama Mann ordered me a new dress for the Enon "dinner on the ground" each year. Oh it may not have been every year, but one year I remember that she ordered me a pastel striped dress."

In March 2000 a niece, Margaret Mann Griffin, had this recollection of her. "Aunt Maggie had to have her face powder, and if she didn't have it she would get sick so she would have to go to the doctor so she could get her powder. She knew if she complained and had to go to the doctor, she would be able to get her powder."

Her son Victor's children, Martha, Dorothy, Virginia and Bubber remembered her in May 2000 and her love of liquor and "dope." Martha remembered that they would take the "dope" capsules and put sugar in them.

## End of Life

Mama Mann died at our home on August 25, 1955. Floyd and Maggie Compton Mann are buried in the Enon Methodist Church Cemetery in Carroll County, Mississippi.

Part 2 C: Allen Ethelior "Thelia" was born in Carroll County, Mississippi, on October 31, 1863, during the American Civil War and during the presidential administration of Abraham Lincoln. This great aunt of mine seemed more like a grandmother to me than her sister, Maggie, who was my grandmother.

Her sister called her Thelia, my mother called her Aunt Thelia, and her grand nieces and nephews called her the endearing name of "Cedy [pronounced seed-e]."

Her family was her sister Maggie's family, and she lived with them for many years. She was their handmaiden, and she spoiled all of them, according to my mother. This caused Mother to think that she had this easy and carefree childhood since Cedy did most of the day-to-day house work and most, if not all, of the cooking.

For an unknown reason, she went blind. After going blind, she continued to help with the chores at home. Later she broke her leg and never was able to walk again. This didn't keep her from participating in various chores such as shelling peas, stringing snap beans, and other small chores. She was always independent with feeding herself, and until the end of her life, she was awake and alert and her mind seemed good until the day she died.

## Other Folks Remember Her

In May 2000, my cousins and her grandnieces and nephew, Martha Mann Bailey, Dorothy Mann Carpenter, Virginia Mann Shaw, and Bubber Mann remembered that she was a very hard worker. Dorothy remembered, "She was always cooking, and she offered everyone something to eat." Ginger remembered, "She was a good person and someone I was glad to have around." Bubber remembered, "She dipped snuff and would use a small stick from a black gum tree to place a 'hit' [his words], between her lip and gums."

Martha remembered, "The grandchildren would be called upon to prepare the little stick by peeling a small portion of the bark off of a small limb of a tree. We would then have to chew one end to make it soft and pliable. She would use this little stick to dip the snuff out of the container to be placed into the inside of the lower lip of her mouth."

On January 26, 2002, my sister Sarah remembered Cedy in this way. "She did all of the cooking in her sister's home and she had a mean streak." We agreed that this mean streak had to do with her belief in discipline.

On May 17, 2002, my brother, Billy, called from Columbus, Mississippi and said, "She was bedridden and blind, but she still was able to interact with people. Daddy didn't like her. Mother said it was because when you [that's me this book's author] were a baby, Cedy was from the old school and would chew your food and give it to you." We both remembered that she was a Baptist. Mother said she was a hard shell Baptist, and we thought of that as a foot-washing Baptist.

## End of Life

Cedy died on March 14, 1956, the night before I was to make my high school senior trip. I don't remember being sad or crying at all and, in fact, I feel sadder today as I write this than I recall feeling that day. She died without anyone missing her. Yet she had contributed so much to her sister Maggie's family. She is buried in the Enon Methodist Church Cemetery in Carroll County beside her sister, Maggie.

**Thelia Compton with grand niece Bobbie Ann Mann**

# Chronology

| | |
|---|---|
| 1863 | Allen Ethelior "Cedy" Compton, daughter of Allen G. and Narcissor Trotter, was born on October 31, 1863 in Carroll County, Mississippi. |
| 1879 | Maggie Bell Compton, daughter of Allen G. and Narcissor Elmyria Trotter Compton, was born on February 14, 1879, in Carroll County, Mississippi. The year of her birth Frank W. Woolworth opened his first successful five-and-ten-cent store in Lancaster, Pennsylvania. |
| 1880 | Floyd Fletcher Mann, son of John Wishum and Sarah Collier Mann, was born on July 29, 1880, in Carroll County, Mississippi. |
| 1886 | Thomas Anderson Noe, [later changed to Noah] son of Robert Dugan and Sarah Ellen Sandlin Noe, was born on June 25, 1886, in Lamar County, Alabama. The year of his birth the Statue of Liberty was dedicated in New York. |
| 1893 | Willie Mae Randall, daughter of Jesse and Annie Johnson Randall, was born on June 5, 1893, in Carroll County, Mississippi. The year of her birth the Ferris wheel made its debut at the Columbian Exposition in Chicago. It was also the year of the first successful gasoline-powered automobile in the United States. |
| 1911 | Thomas Anderson Noah and Willie Mae Randall were married on December 13, 1911, in Carroll County, Mississippi. That year was a historic year for sports. Jim Thorpe, whose tribal name was Bright Path, playing for the Carlisle Indian School made four field goals and seventy yard touchdown run leaving Harvard red-faced. A year later Jim Thorpe made the Americans proud when he took the pentathlon and decathlon trophies at the Olympics. The other big sport's name of the year was Ty Cobb. At that time he had the most times at bat, most hits, most runs, and most stolen bases. |
| 1961 | Tom and Willie Mae Randall Noah celebrated their fiftieth wedding anniversary. |

# Chapter 4  Parents: Robert Randall and Susie Evelyn "Dollie" Mann Noah

Part 1 A: Robert Randall Noah, my father, was born on December 13, 1914, in the Blackmonton Community of Carroll County, Mississippi. He was the second child of his parents, Tom Anderson and Willie Mae Randall Noah. His older brother, William Cade, died at a young age. Therefore, growing up Daddy was the oldest child in this family of eight children. Mother and Daddy were both born 1914. Woodrow Wilson, the twenty-eighth president of the United States, was in office. In that year there were 92,228,496 United States citizens. At the time of Daddy's death in 1997, there were 248,718,301. In those 83 years of his life, the population of the United States increased 37 percent.

On July 03, 1937, Robert Randall Noah from the Blackmonton Community of Carroll County, Mississippi, married Susie Evelyn "Dollie" Mann who was from the Enon Community of Carroll County. Both of these communities are too small to be on a Mississippi State map. They were married in Carroll County in the parsonage of the Black Hawk Methodist Church. I know that mother wore a navy crepe dress, as she held on to this dress for many years.

On June 13, 1997, Louise Lee Jones, a neighbor of Daddy's family and a friend of Daddy's sister, Mary Ellen, gave this account of how Mother and Daddy were introduced on the telephone. "I was dating Lloyd Carpenter from the Enon Community and I met Dollie through Lloyd, who was also from the Enon Community. I remember spending time with Dollie during the week of the Enon Methodist Church Revival, and we walked to church with our boyfriends. Later I introduced Robert—our families were neighbors—to Dollie. Robert and Dollie got married, but Lloyd and I did not." It was Louise's mother, Mrs. Ed Lee, who gave Mother and Daddy a Depression Glass cake plate as a wedding present.

On the day after Mother's funeral, Dell Lee, Daddy's first cousin, gave this account of my parents' wedding day. "I was at my grandfather's house. I saw that Robert was dressed up, and I asked Auntie [Dell's and Daddy's aunt] what was going on, and Auntie said that Robert was going to get married."

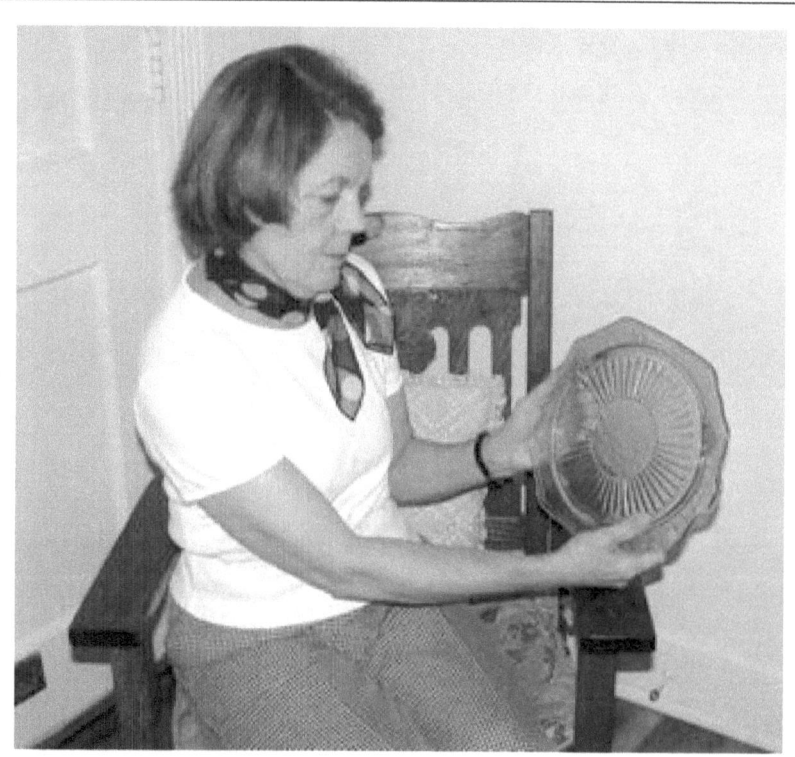
Carolyn Noah Graetz with plate given as a wedding gift to her parents Robert and Dollie Mann Noah by Mrs. Ed Lee, a neighbor of Robert's parents. Photo March 2003

**Robert and Dollie Mann Noah**

I never heard of any kind of celebration following the wedding, and as far as I know they returned home to Daddy's parents and lived there until they moved into the little house across the hollow from them.

From their wedding day forward they continued to live in Carroll County, in the communities of Blackmonton and Old Salem and later in the small town of Vaiden. In the late 1980s, Daddy was placed in the Winona Manor Nursing Home in Winona, Mississippi. There he remained until his death.

Daddy continued to farm with his father, on his father's land. After we moved from his father's place, we moved onto his grandfather's property, later to his uncle's place and back to his father's place again. He never owned any farmland of his own.

During his lifetime Daddy did lots of laborious work. There was no harder working man in the community than Daddy when he was a young man. From his Mother he learned the meaning of working from sunup until sun down.

His main occupation was farming, but he also worked for the WPA—Workman's Progress Association—a President Franklin Roosevelt created job program to help bring the country out of the great Depression, hauled pulpwood, and he worked as a farm hand. Later in life, Daddy worked for one of the Carroll County Supervisors and he helped others do construction work.

Daddy's siblings called him "Bubber" and, that along with his birth name is inscribed on his tombstone. All of his children called him Daddy.

In his youth, Daddy was a handsome young man with curly black hair. In this photograph you can see that is so. In the mid 1990s, Daddy's first cousin, Mae Rae Simpson Garner, told me that Daddy as a young man reminded her of Robert Mitchum, a movie star. In his youth, Daddy joined the Old Salem Presbyterian Church. But he rarely went to church with the family. He did sometimes go to funerals. When he mentioned God, he called him the "Old Master."

Neither of my parents were high school graduates. Daddy attended the Blackmonton County School through eighth grade. Because there were no school buses for transportation to high school in Vaiden, he stayed in the town of Vaiden with folks near the school so he could walk to school. In 1996 I asked Daddy what grade he finished. He told me the eleventh grade. I don't know whether Daddy liked school. He never talked about school and never asked me about my own school. He never looked at or signed my report card. I never saw him read a book, but he did read the local weekly newspaper, and I often saw him reading other newspapers later in life.

Daddy was a strict disciplinarian when I grew up, and I was afraid of him. In many ways he was a misunderstood man, but I had no trouble understanding his expectations of me.

His discipline could be tough, and I wanted to stay clear of his anger. If you got him angry, there was no reasoning with him, nor did I try. We were not given the opportunity to explain ourselves. He knew only one kind of discipline, and that was whippings or lickings, and he sometimes used the words "wear you out or tear you up." Daddy whipped with his bare hand, a belt, a razor strap, or a nice limb from a tree. He didn't allow us to cry after he whipped us. We weren't allowed to even sniffle. Yet in later life, I never held that against him. It was just the way it was.

I tried to make sure I didn't test his limits. At least, that is true to a point, but I did like to eat green plums, and for Daddy that was something not to be done. If my memory serves me correctly, he was afraid of green plums because he thought they caused colitis. His older brother, Cade, had died at a young age with colitis, I was told. If we ate green plums and Daddy found out about it, the standard treatment was a dose of castor oil. That was terrible stuff. I could not stand to smell it, and just the thought of it always seemed awful then and now.

Another no-no was tree climbing. But it was fun to climb trees, and sometimes we threw caution to the wind and climbed trees anyway. However, we didn't brag about it. We knew if we did climb a tree, and he found out about it the consequence was a good whipping. We call it a spanking today. Yet, as an adult I realize climbing trees was a sensible fear of his. None of us ever got a broken bone and that was good. Expense for a doctor would have been a burden.

Other whippings occurred when my sister, Sarah, and I would get into fights, big fights. I was older and bigger than she was, so I think I usually won the fight. But if Mother told Daddy about a fight, he whipped both of us.

I remember on one occasion when we had just moved back into my grandparents' house at Blackmonton. Billy, Sarah, and I wandered off to the neighbor's unattended house. The neighbor, Mr. Ed Lee, had moved, but not completely. Being adventurous and curious, we went there. There were not any locks on the doors so we made a tour, but we didn't bother anything in the unlocked house. On our way home, Daddy met us in the road and whipped Sarah and me. Billy was excused. He was only four years old.

I have no grudge to nurse as a result of Daddy's discipline approach. He had learned this method of discipline growing up, and it was the accepted method. Child psychology was unknown to rural people in those days.

I think he mellowed when my brothers got old enough to test him. After leaving home for good in late summer 1956, I, too, was not as inclined to fear him and, if memory serves me right, I had no further discipline problems. My relationship with Daddy was neither warm nor cold. I think he loved me, and I always loved him despite his faults and his type of discipline.

Daddy didn't have many people he called friends. But there were many country and small town people who were family friends, who would have said they were Daddy's friend.

In Carroll County, Mississippi, there were two county seats. Creating two county seats was a way of appeasing Vaiden and keeping that part of Carroll County from forming a new county. Carrollton was the other county seat. Carrollton had a sheriff and Vaiden had a deputy sheriff. Daddy had a strong opinion about who was elected deputy sheriff. On one occasion the candidate for deputy sheriff was Herman "Chargie" Michie. A hotheaded man shot him. Chargie didn't die, but the news spread far and wide.

Daddy did love politics, but he disliked many people in politics. At home he would curse certain folks. I'm not sure what Daddy would have done if one of the people he disliked had shown up at the door when he was "raising cane" which is what Mother called it. That never happened, but I think he may have walked off.

He had a biased opinion about politics and would have been called a Yellow Dog Democrat in his early life. This meant that he would have voted for a yellow dog before he would have voted outside of the Democratic Party. At that time and until General Dwight D. Eisenhower was elected president in 1952, most Southern states were solidly Democratic, and there were probably many Yellow Dog Democrats because the Southern people had considered Franklin D. Roosevelt a savior when he brought out various programs to get the United States out of the Great Depression.

Ultimately it was World War II that got us out of the Depression as much as it was Roosevelt's WPA and CCC programs. But many Southerners blamed the Depression on President Herbert Hoover, a Republican, and to them Franklin D. Roosevelt, a Democrat, had saved our country.

It was the beat supervisor's race that Daddy really did get what I would call nuts about. My grandfather Tom Noah ran for beat supervisor at least once. I don't know if Daddy campaigned for him or not or how they campaigned, but I do remember that Daddy did not like Mr. Walter Moses, who worked for Mr. Weldon Baskin, who became supervisor. Prior to legalized whiskey in Mississippi, Daddy made bootleg whiskey with his great uncle Luther Noah. He made it and he drank it. He drank it straight out of the bottle, in fact, he guzzled it.

When our family moved from the Heggie Place back to Blackmonton in 1948, he escaped Uncle Luther's bootlegging, but he had neither desire nor ability to escape the clutches of whiskey. He continued to make batches for himself to drink. Later in life he bought that contraband other bootleggers made or got it from package stores once liquor was legalized in Mississippi. Undisputedly, alcohol destroyed any incentive that he had to work, to have fun, to be a family man, to provide for his family, or to enjoy life. It, also, destroyed any pride he had in his appearance.

It caused loads of conflict and torment in our family because Mother thought Daddy could just stop drinking. It didn't help that Mother epitomized the life long teetotaler. I don't even think she wanted to moisten a fruitcake with liquor.

Daddy certainly had good qualities, but I can say that his alcohol problem made Mother's life and the life of his children miserable at times. I have come to realize that Mother was a strong woman to put up with Daddy's drinking behavior for so long. On October 12, 2000, I was talking to my sister and asked her something that she remembered about Daddy. She said, "I can remember Daddy would come in drunk and this would cause Mother to get upset. I would lie down on the floor with him to comfort him."

I can also knowingly write that Daddy's mother did a lot of worrying about him. He must have been going through hell and so was his family. Daddy would never have admitted he was an alcoholic and never would have sought help.

In the late 1980s Daddy had a fall and cut his head badly. He had to be taken by ambulance to the hospital in Winona, and from there to the

Baptist Hospital in Jackson to the Drug and Alcohol Treatment Center. I drove up to Mississippi in our Ford van, and my brother, Billy, and I took Daddy to the Drug and Alcohol Treatment Center at the Baptist Hospital in Jackson. They recognized that by now Daddy had organic brain syndrome and that they could not help him.

He never returned home, but was placed in the Winona Manor Nursing Home where he remained the rest of his life. He was there over ten years and adapted pretty well. He stopped drinking and stopped smoking. He did get to come home on visits when my sister, Sarah, or I went to get him when we were in Vaiden.

He never gave us any trouble about returning to the nursing home, and in fact he would call it to our attention that it was time to return to the nursing home. On these short visits, Daddy and Mother did not have a lot of yelling and screaming, but there was not any warmth there either. Mother liked to go to the nursing home to visit, but it was not just because Daddy was there. Many other folks from Vaiden were in that same nursing home and Mother liked to visit them, too.

On one of my visits July 1993, I brought Daddy to Vaiden to spend the night at home on Saturday night, July 17. That night he got up to go to the bathroom, fell, and broke his hip. He was operated on the following Monday, July 19 at the Grenada Hospital in Grenada, Mississippi. I stayed at the hospital during the operation, and his sister, Ruth, was there also.

After a short recovery period in the hospital he went back to the nursing home. He was given physical therapy, but never walked again. He adapted to the wheelchair without any problem.

But I do have some good memories and fortunately I realized that his alcohol problem was a disease. One good memory has to do with Daddy's excitement at Christmas time when I was a young child. On Christmas Eve night we would put out milk and cookies for Santa Claus. We children were then awakened by Daddy after Santa Claus came. We got up and played until we were tired. We then went back to sleep. When I found out about Santa Claus, I missed this part. Mother didn't take to this too well, and in my adulthood I began to understand why. She was probably tired from getting ready for the Christmas meal which took lots of time to prepare and cook, and Daddy never helped even a little bit with preparing, serving, or cleaning up after a meal.

Daddy had some hobbies that he enjoyed in his young life, too. He had friends he would go bird hunting with, and he would kill quail to bring home to eat. His first cousin, Dell Lee, on March 12, 2000, remembered daddy's quail hunting. "I remember him quail hunting with a dog named Kate, and the dog would retrieve the quail and bring it to him while he was on the horse."

Daddy's early brain deterioration and early nursing home placement were a direct result of his lack of self—preservation due to alcohol. I was sadder at Daddy's funeral than at Mother's funeral. Much of that sadness had to do with the life he lived, but also because he never got to enjoy his grandchildren, he seemed so very sad, and that he made Mother's life miserable at times. She probably made his miserable, also, as she had too many bad experiences with alcohol in her birth family and with Daddy.

In this paragraph I will attempt to demonstrate Daddy's memory loss. On November 26, 1994, I sat with him at the table in the Winona Manor Nursing Home, and I asked him how to make whiskey. He gave me this recipe: "You use rye, sugar and water. The water would be heated in a drum then the sugar and rye would be added. This combination would be brought to a boil, and when it got thick it would be placed into a keg." This is as much of a conversation as we could have. Before it was over he became aggravated and wheeled himself away.

That little bit of information from Daddy personally is not meant to hurt or harm him, but is added to demonstrate his loss of interest in any topic. He seemed content to sit in his wheelchair day in and day out in the nursing home. He knew to wheel himself into the dining room for a little cup of coffee in the afternoon, and that was the one pleasure he found in the last days of his life.

I never stopped loving him, but I was concerned about his loss of enthusiasm for life. Thinking about him when he was approximately the age of 58, he had lost his motivation to work, had little interaction with people, was likely depressed, and ate very little saddens me more. I am 65, seven years older than Daddy when he lost his passion for life. I knew this man when I was a child as a hard working man who came from a good family; a family that loved him though was dismayed by his loss of zest for life at a young age.

## Other Folks Remember Him

On July 2, 2002 Sarah Lou Noah Planer, my sister, shared this memory about Daddy. "Daddy and I were in a wagon returning to our home on the Heggie from our grandparents, Tom and Willie Noah. We were traveling on some kind of dirt trail through the woods when the horses got scared and began to run away. Daddy was holding on to me and began yelling 'whoa, whoa, you son-of a gun [gun substituted by the author] whoa, whoa.' He finally got control of the horses again and we made it home safely."

On May 5, 2002 Chuck Planer, his son-in-law, remembered that Daddy was shy and after he got into the nursing home he remembered that Daddy liked to have a watch not only for the time of day but also the date. "I would buy a watch at the Base Exchange (BX) and take him one. He got a new one each time the battery died. That was easier than replacing the battery. He was buried with his watch on his arm."

His granddaughter, Susan Planer Phillips, wrote this contribution on November 26, 2002. "The best thing that I remember about my Grandpa is that he really did love me, and he showed it in his own way. At one time he had a pony. I can remember him helping me ride the pony. When I would say good-bye to him, he had a stiff hug, which I knew was the only way he knew how to hug, and he would slip me any where from a dollar to a five dollar bill into my hand."

**Robert Randall Noah**

**Robert Noah with Grandson Derek Graetz**

**Dollie Noah with Grandchildren Derek and Gionne**

On December 2, 2001, my brother, Billy, remembered Daddy in this way. "Daddy liked to pick at people." He remembered that he made whiskey and drank it with G. A. Pinkston and Rufus Minyard. Another memory of Billy's was that Daddy and a one-armed man, Mr. Hughes, cut pulpwood.

On July 16, 2002, by telephone my brother, Billy, recalled it seemed to him Daddy changed when we moved into Vaiden. He felt that our move into the town of Vaiden away from Daddy's country upbringing separated Daddy from him best country friends. Living in town made it easier for Daddy to get the whiskey that overtook him.

Billy said he would never forget when Daddy opened up to him a little prior to Billy's going into service. "Daddy admitted to me that he had a drinking problem. The Vietnam War was in full swing, and Daddy was seeing his first-born son go to war. Daddy had seen friends go to war in World War II but he had not seen a brother or child go to war. He must have felt afraid."

My additional comment to Billy's regarding Daddy: His first two children—his girls—were already away from home. I was married and living in California when Billy left for Vietnam and Sarah was married and living in Florida.

On April 19, 2002 I asked my brother Bobby what his thoughts were about Daddy. He said. "Our parents did the best they could." He then said that was how he wanted to remember them.

His son, Marvin "Noggin" Noah remembered Daddy in this way on July 5, 2002. "Daddy made sure that I played ball and on Sunday mornings when I had a paper route he would drive me around to deliver the Jackson Daily."

Marsha Shaw Noah, his daughter-in-law, remembered Daddy in this way on July 5, 2002. "He was always very nice to me and when Marvin was in Alaska and I would go there he would try to do things on my car if needed."

His sister, Bobbie Noah Smith, wrote about him on April 18, 2002. Bubber was not as temperamental as Ken, my other brother. He was more laid back. He taught me to drive a stick shift truck as he had more patience than Daddy and Ken."

On January 5, 2004, his grandson, Douglas Planer, remembered. "Grandpa surprised us with a Shetland pony that he called Bullet. The pony did not like to be ridden, and one day I was ridding and Bullet took off running. I also, remember that Grandpa would take us to Piggly-Wiggly and to the toy store. We were allowed to buy one candy bar and a coke at Piggly-Wiggly and one toy at the toy. He, also, let us drive Uncle Bobby's Model T and that was plenty fun."

On July 27, 2004, his grandson, Duane "Tally" Noah remembered Daddy use to sit on the front porch and this would give him the opportunity to play around the pulpwood even through Daddy would yell at Tally and Holley fearing they would get hurt. "Grandpa regularly read the newspaper." Tally gave this account of him accidentally shooting Daddy with his cousin Douglas's BB gun. Tally and his family along with Mother and Daddy were visiting the Planers in Panama City, Florida. "I was about six years old. I told Grandpa if he came any closer I was going to shoot him. He told me to put that gun down. I shot him. I remember that the shot did hit him but I don't remember what happened to me."

Daddy's sister-in-law, Louise Eades Noah, remembered Daddy in this way on April 20, 2002. "Your daddy came into this world working, and he never stopped until his drinking got the best of him."

## End of Life

Daddy died on March 24, 1997, in the Tyler-Holmes Memorial Hospital in Winona Mississippi. He was 82 years old. His heart had given out. His funeral service was held at the Oliver Funeral in Winona, Mississippi.

Robert and Dollie Mann Noah are buried in the Vaiden Cemetery.

In the weekly newspaper, *The Conservative* I wrote about my dad for the May 27, 1997, issue. Much of the information in that article is already in this book. It is entitled "Memories of Dad Are Still With Me." The article follows.

It was a little over two years ago that I wrote about my mother, Dollie Mann Noah and her life in Carroll County, Mississippi. It is only fitting to do the same for my father who died at the Tyler-Holmes Hospital in Winona, Mississippi on March 24, 1997.

My dad was a Carroll Countian his entire life until he went to the Winona Manor Nursing Home. At various times he called home the communities of Blackmonton, Old Salem, the town of Vaiden, and at one time his mailing address was Coila.

He was the first generation, on his father Tom Noah's side, to be born in Mississippi, but his mother, Willie Mae Randall Noah's ancestry reaches back to the 1830s when her great-grandfather, Samuel Johnson came to Carroll County from Warren County, Mississippi. Samuel Johnson and his wife Patsy had many children. One was Gilbert Johnson. Gilbert was a Confederate soldier in the Civil War and is buried in the Old Salem Cemetery along side his wife, Emily Blakely Johnson. Their child, Annie Johnson, married Jesse Randall in 1892, and their first child, Willie Mae Randall Noah, was my dad's mother.

Daddy was the second oldest child of Tom and Willie Randall Noah. He and my mother, Dollie Mann, were married on July 3, 1937, at the Black Hawk Methodist Parsonage.

From my dad and his family I learned much, but the importance of hard work was one of the earliest things that I learned. As a young man there was no harder worker than my dad. He would go to bed with the chickens, but he got up before daybreak and worked from sun up until sun down. He never, ever, complained or bragged about the hard work he did as a young man, nor did he ever talk about how good his children had it in comparison to the hard work he did in the early part of his life.

When I was a child, my dad was a strict disciplinarian. He had a fear of green plums, and we sometimes ate them anyway. If he found out about it, it meant a large dose of castor oil. He also didn't want us to climb trees. He was afraid we would fall out of the tree and break an arm or a leg. Living out in the country without a telephone, transportation, or the ready availability of a doctor could, indeed, create many problems and my dad knew this.

In my dad's final days it was his sisters, Ruth Noah Eddins and Ruby Noah Jones, who went to see him most every week. As with many funerals, Daddy's was sort of a homecoming for our family. All five of his children were there, and so were all six of his grandchildren. His sister, Ruby Jones, Bobbie Smith, and Ruth Eddins were there as were all of their children. His brother, Ken Noah, died in the early 1960s, but Ken's wife, Louise and son Kenneth Ray were there.

This family must love Mississippi as none have moved more than one and one-half hours drive from Carroll County except my sister, Sarah Planer who lives in Oklahoma City, Oklahoma and me. I live in New Orleans, Louisiana. My three brothers all live in Mississippi.

It has been almost 56 years since I've called Carroll County home, but until my dad died I would still say to everyone, I'm going home. Now what do I say? I guess I'll have to say I'm going back to my roots, to see some relatives, or to have a rest and relaxation period from the hustle and bustle of city life. For whatever reason, I'll always call Vaiden my hometown.

Part 1 B: Susie Evelyn "Dollie" Mann Noah my mother was born in the Enon Community of Carroll County, Mississippi, on June 7, 1914. Her parents were Floyd Fletcher and Maggie Bell Compton Mann. She was their fourth and last child. Though her birth name was Susie Evelyn, and she sometimes called herself by that name, she was known as Dollie by everyone. I don't think more than two dozen people knew Mother's birth name. On her tombstone both Susie Evelyn and "Dollie" are inscribed.

Enon, the small community where she was born, was hallowed ground to my mother. If this were not so during her childhood and early adulthood, she would certainly have consecrated it after she left there in 1937. A visit to Enon was like a journey back to her heart's desire. Her roots were there. Both sets of her grandparents had lived there, and one set of her great—grandparents was part of the Enon Community.

She especially had strong emotional ties to the Enon Methodist Church. She found her sustenance there. She loved to take her children to events at that church. I especially remember the revival weeks and the "dinners on the ground" now called Homecoming. On Saturday afternoon before the Enon event, Mother was busily cooking and getting our clothes in proper order. We usually would get a new outfit, the first one of the summer, for that event.

For many years—even in my adult life—when I returned to that Enon Church for various events I was reminded of a time when I got lost from Mother. Everyone was looking for me, thinking that I may be in the Pulushi Creek that was nearby. It caused a panic, but I was found under the church.

I have lived in New Orleans since 1956 and Mother is dead over five years, yet I will be attending the Enon Homecoming in two weeks, the fourth Sunday in May, 2000.

I wrote, "Today May 28, 2000, I attended another Homecoming at the Enon Methodist Church. I could not help but think about how my mother loved this place. I also felt my own emotional tie to this place where my great-grandfather, John Mann, built the pulpit.

"At least three of Mother's Mann first cousins were there today. I felt Mother's presence at the Homecoming. I felt my spirits uplifted singing the hymns and had a mental picture my grandfather, Floyd Mann, and his brothers in the choir. I never saw them sit in any other place."

The Enon Church cemetery brings the emotional ties even closer. In this cemetery are the graves of one set of my grandparents, Floyd and Maggie Compton Mann; two sets of great-grandparents, John and Sarah Collier Mann and Allen and Narcissor Trotter Compton; and one set of great-great grandparents, John and Abigail Tisdale Collier. There are an aunt and uncle, Victor and Vera Wilshire Mann, and another uncle, Percy Mann. Great-uncles and aunts are too many to count but to name a few Turner and Lola Carpenter Mann, Grenade and Lena Johnson Mann, Walter Mann, and other Mann great-uncles. My great-great uncle Luther Noah and his wife Betty Pinkston Noah and their children are, buried there. My great aunt Thelia Compton is buried there next to her sister. These ties bind me to this land as they did my mother.

Mother joined this Methodist church in her youth and remained a member until the 1950s. Sarah, my sister and I became members of the Shongalo Presbyterian Church in 1955 and Mother joined that church shortly afterward. We never talked about her changing her denomination from Methodist to Presbyterian. I do know she never regretted the switch, that she was loved the Presbyterian Church and the people in it. However, she never lost her love for the church she was so closely allied with in her youth.

She attended the Enon Country School from the first through the eighth grade. One of her teachers at Enon was Gertie Brisindine. In the ninth grade she went to high school in Carrollton, but there were no school buses to get her into town so she had to board with someone. On March 18, 1994, Mother remembered two special friends of her youth and school at Carrollton, Ida Johnson and Agnes McGregor. By this date she was recovering from her broken hip and gave no other details.

On May 5, 2002, I was able to contact Agnes McGregor McArthur in Jackson, Mississippi, where she has lived since 1936. She was delighted to hear from me and reminisced about times with Mother. "We roomed together at my Aunt Ida Johnson's in Carrollton in the ninth grade. My family lived out in the country near New Salem and Dollie's family lived near Enon. On Sunday afternoon we went into Carrollton. We attended school Monday through Friday, and on Friday afternoon we went home to our families for the weekend. I just loved Dollie. We had such a good time together. At Aunt Ida's we had all three of our meals. We could walk to school and we walked to Aunt Ida's for lunch every day. My family paid Aunt Ida in produce and I think Dollie's family did the same."

**Dollie Mann**

Ida's family moved to Weir, Mississippi, and Mother started the tenth grade in Carrollton, but for some reason she did no go any further. It is likely that it was too much of a financial burden on the family. However, Mother harbored no insecurities as a result of her lack of education. She could talk with anyone who would talk with her. In this way, I am surely like my mother. My daughter never meets a stranger either.

Mother never educated me about the "facts of life," but one of my aunts, Daddy's sister, Bobbie Noah Smith told me that my mother did educate her about the "facts of life." Neither my parents, grandparents, aunts, and uncles or anyone else ever used the word sex in front of us during my childhood or young adulthood when talking about the "facts of life." If the word pregnancy was used, it was in hushed tones.

From mother I definitely knew I was not to get pregnant, and I knew she was talking about abstinence. That was the only thing Mother knew about birth control. I do remember that on one occasion I was going some place with Mother and Daddy, and they wanted to talk about someone who was pregnant. They couldn't find words to talk about it without saying the word pregnant. Somehow in a round—about way I understood that someone was going to have a baby. I vaguely remember that my sister and I recognized when people were pregnant and we talked about it between the two of us.

My youngest brother, Marvin, was born in 1953. I was 14 years old, and I knew Mother was pregnant, but Mother never talked to me about the fact we were going to have an addition to our family. But I do remember when Mother went into labor, Daddy went to get John Lester Stuart, a neighbor, to take Mother into Vaiden to my grandparents' home where Mother gave birth to my baby brother, Marvin.

I did have some curiosity about sex, but none that I ever verbally quizzed anyone about. But I did learn from the farm animals. I saw dogs running after dogs and having sex; I saw bulls running after cows and having sex; I saw male pigs running after the female and having sex, I saw birds having sex; and I saw the roosters chasing hens and having sex. That was the extent of my sex education.

This didn't mean that I was free of sexual thoughts and at the age of 12 or 13, I was attracted to the opposite sex. I imagined being married and having children, I played paper dolls, and those paper dolls had a home with a mother, father, and children. It was at the age of 17 when I went to nursing school that I began learning about the human anatomy of the sex organs. I knew mothers were pregnant, but how that baby got out of the mother wasn't known to me until nursing school.

Mother didn't hold grudges. Really in her heart she had a song, and could get a high spirit with the smallest encouragement. Mother could get tickled over some little thing and she and I would laugh until it hurt. She liked to dance, to sing in church, and to play cards. Later in life she enjoyed television and the freedom to walk up to town in Vaiden as long as there was a town.

Her frustrations were expressed in such expressions as "Lord knows what, Lordy Moses what to do now, good God almighty, gosh darn it," or some simple saying like "aw doodly squat." Still other expressions were "good golly Miss Molly" and "Lord only knows" or "Lord, have mercy." She could be very sensitive if I corrected her. She said things like "I'm madder than a setting hen." Vividly in my mind and in the mind of my daughter, Gionne is a time when we were in Vaiden, and we were driving around. Mother said something about a book in the liberry. I corrected her and explained it was lie' brer-e, trying to explain it to her phonetically, and she got furious with me so furious that I had to take her home to let her settle. A week or two later she wrote me that a well known lady in town had helped her to pronounce library correctly and she thought that lady was doing her a favor.

After the five of us children grew up, Mother loved to spend time with her children. She loved the attention that she received from us, especially from her girls. But Mother was never reluctant to let us know we were not perfect. She didn't hold her tongue one little bit if she was fretted with us.

Some of my best memories of my mother have to do with visits I made to Vaiden with my children. During those visits to Vaiden she became our constant companion. I can still hear her voice when we arrived at her home in Vaiden. She would come out and tell us how glad she was to see us. This she did over and over, and it is something that I miss when I go to Vaiden these days.

Mother broke her leg on March 11, 1994. She was never able to live in her home again. Though her leg mended, her mind got worse. She gave up, and was placed in the Winona Manor Nursing Home. Nursing Home placement was always part of her plan, and she didn't mind going there.

The only house my parents ever owned was sold soon after we realized that Mother would never live at home again. After selling the house we five children divided the furniture and other family treasures. My parents had furniture from mother's family including a china cabinet that mother's grandfather, John Wishum Mann, built, a bedroom set that belonged to Daddy's parents, and an iron bed that belonged to Daddy's uncle and aunt. Each one of us came to treasure bits and pieces of furniture that drifted down from one generation to another. However, all of us were committed to never clash over any of my parents' possessions, and all of us have kept that commitment.

Here is my own account of the last time I was with my mother before she died. I recorded it in her hospital room at the Tyler-Holmes Hospital in Winona, Mississippi, on November 26, 1994. "In the hospital room with my mother, she mostly sleeps and then sleeps some more. Every now and then she opens her eyes, and I ask her how she is doing? She responds 'I'm OK.' When asked if she is comfortable, she says she is. Infrequently she awakens and will be able to answer a few simple questions with some prodding."

I made another recording early the next morning in the visitor's lounge. "Last night I spent the night in my mother's hospital room. It doesn't feel like I got much sleep as the nursing staff came often into her room with medication, to turn her, to check her vital signs and the infusion. Mother kept bending her arm with the infusion so the beeper went off."

"As I sit here in the visitor's lounge seemingly in half stupor, I reflect on my mother's life and what it was like. She loved to go any and everywhere. She especially, loved church and never questioned her faith." The next morning Mother seemed a little perkier, so I left for home.

## Other Folks Remember Her

On January 26, 2002, my sister, Sarah, recalled some of Mother's actions and reactions. "Mother didn't believe in cursing. The first time she heard me say shit I was using a hammer and I know exactly where I was. I was standing under the little corner built-in cabinet at Blackmonton when I hit my finger with the hammer. I said shit and she slapped me." Per Sarah, "Mother never said shit except to say, 'shit, shit, double shit' and that to her was taking care of the situation."

My sister shared one funnier story about our mother. "Mother was in Selma, Alabama, with Chuck and me April 1968 awaiting the arrival of my daughter, Susan. We went to eat at Morrison's Cafeteria. There was a large mirror where we were standing in line. Mother said, 'I do believe I see a set of twins.' When we realized what Mother saw was a child in the mirror, we both got really tickled. Chuck wanted to deny that he knew us, we were laughing so hard."

On July 5, 2002, my brother, Billy, recalled memories of our mother. "I inherited a quick temper, but like my mother I don't hold a grudge."

On that same day another brother, Marvin remembered Mother in this way. "Mother made me go to Sunday School every Sunday. She began preparation on Saturday night by reminding me that tomorrow was Sunday. On Sunday morning she would get up at daylight and begin slamming doors making sure to wake me up."

Recalling our mother in other ways, we were reminded of Mother's hard work. She got up every morning early and cooked breakfast before all of us left for school, and during the summer she still got up early and cooked breakfast. She made homemade biscuits and cooked scrambled eggs. We had buttered biscuits with molasses sometimes made out of sorghum cane. After school we usually had a snack and Sarah especially remembers the baked sweet potatoes.

Susan Planer Phillips, her granddaughter, wrote this about Mother on November 26, 2002. "The best thing that I remember about my Grandma is that she was always singing. She would sing in the kitchen when she was cooking or cleaning, and she would sing throughout the house. She sang mostly gospel songs, but she sang some of the classic country, too. On our trips to Vaiden when our visits came to an end, we had to travel many miles back to Oklahoma, and she would cry. We cried, too." In the last sentence of that note from Susan, "I loved my grandparents, and I love the fact that I have these memories that they loved me, too."

Mother's first cousin, Margaret Mann Griffin, shared memories of my mother in 2001. One thing that she recalled is that they rented the movie, *Home Alone,* and during the movie Mother kept saying "You're leaving him, you're leaving him," as if she could get the attention of the family in the movie who was leaving their son alone.

Her son-in-law, Charles "Chuck" Planer, remembered her in this way. "She was able to put up with her children's comings and goings and always wanted to go along even when not invited."

Another memory of his had to do with Mary Kalvert, the CPA for Chuck and Sarah. "Dollie was spending some time with us in Oklahoma, and Mary, a fellow Mississippian, was coming over to our house to meet her. When Mary walked into the front door, Dollie stood up and the introduction was made. Mary said 'Dollie welcome to Oklahoma,' and Dollie replied, 'my, you are a plump one.' However, the rest of the visit went well."

Her sister-in-law, Bobbie Noah Smith, remembered her on April 18, 2002. Dollie was like another sister when she and Bubber married. I was ten years old, and she taught me about 'mother nature.'"

## End of Life

One month to the day after I wrote the above account at the hospital, Mother died peacefully in her sleep on December 26, 1994. When my brother, Billy, called to tell me of her death, I was finishing paper work for my job and was planning a trip to see her within the next few days.

Her death certificate gives the cause of her death as a cardiac arrest. Other diagnoses included coronary insufficiency, cerebrovascular insufficiency, and chronic organic brain syndrome. Her funeral was held at the Shongalo Presbyterian Church on my fifty-sixth birthday, December 29, of that year.

Mother made funeral plans easy for us. We knew the funeral home to contact with a partially pre-paid plan and she had arranged for my brother, Bobby, to buy several plots in the Vaiden Cemetery many years earlier. Mother had made the most of a tough, hard life.

The funeral service was held at the Shongalo Presbyterian Church in Vaiden. She had been a member there almost forty years. I gave the eulogy, entitled "O Mother of Mine."

You all know that I've come here with a heavy heart today, but I would like to say good-bye to my mother in a public way. God, as we know and believe, is everywhere. But God knew he needed someone to assist him. And so he made mothers. But, let us not forget that God made fathers, also.

For eighty years my mother was needed here on earth to do God's work, and all of us know my mother took this mission seriously. But, O Mother of Mine, how we will miss you.

But Mother in so many ways, by the life you have lived, you have made your death easier for us. My only wish is that I could have written down some funny stories told about you in the last couple of days. And by the way, though Daddy may not know, he is fortunate that you've gone ahead and paved the way for him.

Of course, Mother, we know was not without her faults. We are all sinners. But, I believe your good traits overshadow those faults, and that you'll be remembered for your love of God, your unquestioning faith, your love of people and theirs of you, your jolliness, and most of all for your love to go out and be with people. Even in these last few months of your life, and especially on one occasion that I remember. You were in the Tyler-Holmes Hospital in Winona and you said to me. "Well just look at me, I've come off without my shoes." And in the next breath you said, "Let's go out to Ruby's."

O Mother of Mine, let us not forget some of those lessons you taught us about life: to make the best out of difficult situations, to never hold grudges, to be forgiving, and also always, always expect more out of your children than of others. Those lessons are truly valuable.

And so, O Mother of Mine, I bid you farewell and good-bye for all of us. With the promise that I will work on being kind to my family, my friends, and even to strangers I meet. And I hope others will do likewise.

After mother's funeral that day my sister and I went to the nursing home to collect her possessions and to say good-bye to the staff. Shoni Montgomery, one of mother's caregivers at the nursing home, gave this account of her death. "On the night of her death, Marie Brown gave "Miss Dollie" a snack. Later her vital signs were normal, but her breathing had increased. Dr. Middleton was called, and oxygen was started. In less than ten minutes I went back into her room and she was gone."

My first Mother's Day May 1995 without my mother prompted me to write about her life in *The Conservative*, the weekly newspaper, that I read growing up and my family had read for generations. It was entitled: "Remembering My Mother and Her Life in Carroll County." Much of this article is a repetition of the information previously written.

My mother was born in 1914 in the small community of Enon in Carroll County, Mississippi. Her parents, Floyd and Maggie Bell Compton Mann, gave her the name of Susie Evelyn Mann. However, everyone knew her as "Dollie." In fact, on her tombstone we have both "Dollie" and Susie Evelyn Mann so that descendent hunters, like me, will not be trying to figure out if "Dollie" and Susie Evelyn is the same person.

When she married my father, Robert Noah, in 1937 she moved away from Enon, but she was always a resident of Carroll County except for the last few months of her life. And her love for Enon, especially the Enon Methodist Church, and the people of that small community was always present. When we would travel from Vaiden to Enon, my mother would announce when we arrived at a certain place in the road that she got this special thrill knowing she was back in the territory of her birth and childhood. I now know exactly what she meant as I experience that same feeling when I cross the Mississippi line on Interstate-55 en route from New Orleans to Vaiden.

Her family had been part of the Enon community for three generations. Her grandfather, John Wishum Mann, built the pulpit at that little church, and had been part of the Enon church singing school in 1911. His children Floyd, Dell, and Turner all sang in the choir at Enon.

On my last trip to the Enon Homecoming, I could still see those three men in the choir, and oh, how they could sing. It was at Enon that my mother learned to sing those old familiar church hymns. She had some she especially loved. At her funeral, we sang "When the Roll is Called up Yonder." This hymn was selected by my brother, Billy, who knew it was one of her favorites. I would have said "In the Sweet By and By." In the Presbyterian Church that I belong to today we don't sing either of these songs very much, but if I hear them, I'll feel my mother's presence.

She really did believe those were the easy times, and she was never reluctant to tell her five children that it was not easy to raise us. She also never hesitated to let us know when she thought we were doing something wrong.

The last time that I saw my mother alive was the Sunday after Thanksgiving in 1994. She was in the Tyler-Holmes Hospital, and very sick. I knew I was seeing and attending her final hours.

I spent the night in her hospital room on Saturday night. But the next day she perked up, so I took this opportunity to encourage her to eat and to exercise her contracted hand. She didn't like this and she said to me, "No matter what, that nurse will come out in you." She wasn't being complimentary, either. She was letting me know how she felt, and in particular that I was mean to try to get her to do something that she didn't want to do.

For my mother, each of her five children had a different part to play in her life after we grew up and left home. My youngest brother, Marvin, lived in Vaiden, and was always called upon to do the every day thing. It was his wife, Marsha, who was called upon to escort her via ambulance to a Jackson hospital the day she broke her leg. When she got scared to stay alone, she knew she had a place to go overnight.

It was my brother Bobby who sent her flowers for Valentine's Day, and my brother Billy whom she always aimed to please, cooking those vegetables and cornbread. It was my sister, Sarah, who, although living the farthest away in Oklahoma City, took the most responsibility for mother's needs. She was at my mother beck and call, and some of us thought she spoiled my mother. As they say, she was doing her thing.

As for me, I always felt like I did my part and could be called upon for any and every thing. However, yard work was my specialty, and each and every visit included it. For most of the forty years that I was away, my mother and I wrote or talked on the telephone weekly, and I loved getting the Vaiden news. The memories of my mother will go with me the rest of my life. As one can tell, there are so many memories about my mother's life to share, and it is my wish that sharing this will cause others to remember her in some special way.

# Chronology

1914     Susie Evelyn "Dollie" Mann, daughter of Floyd Fletcher and Maggie Bell Compton Mann, was born on June 7, 1914, in the Enon Community of Carroll County, Mississippi. The year of her of her birth World War I began following the assassination of the Austrian Archduke Francis Ferdinand and his wife Sophie by a Serbian Nationalist in Sarajevo, Bosnia. Following this assassination Austria declared war on Serbia. Germany declared war on Russia and France, and Britain declared war on Germany. This series of events led to the outbreak of World War I in 1917.

1914     Robert Randall Noah, son of Thomas Anderson "Tom" and Willie Mae Randall Noah, was born in the Blackmonton Community of Carroll County, Mississippi on December 13, 1914.

1914     In this year the Panama Canal was opened after ten years of construction. This waterway across the Isthmus of Panama connected the Atlantic and Pacific Oceans by way of the Caribbean Sea.

1914     First green and red lights were installed in Cleveland, Ohio.

1917     Was the year of the Russian Revolution in which Czar Nicholas II was forced to abdicate in October 1917 the Bolsheviks led by Lenin and Trotsky, seized power in Russia.

1919     After World War I national prohibition became the law when the Eighteenth Amendment to the Constitution of the United States forbidding the manufacture, sale, import, or export of intoxicating liquors was passed. Illicit manufacture of liquor rapidly sprang up and authorities were able to suppress it. In 1933 the Twenty-first Amendment repealed prohibition. However, several states and counties continued prohibition under local option. Mississippi was one of those states. By 1966 no statewide prohibition laws existed.

1920     The Nineteenth Amendment to the United States Constitution passed granting women the right to vote.

1920     On September 17, 1920 the National Football League was organized.

| | |
|---|---|
| 1927 | On May 11, 1927 Airman Charles A. Lindbergh flew his airplane, the Spirit of St. Louis, from New York's Roosevelt Field to the Le Bourget Field in Paris, arriving g on May 12. |
| 1928 | Alexander Fleming discovered penicillin. |
| 1937 | Robert Randall Noah and Susie Evelyn "Dollie" Mann Noah were married on July 3, 1937, in the parsonage of the Black Hawk Methodist Church. That same year King Edward VIII of England voluntarily abdicated his crown to marry Mrs. Wallis Simpson, an American who was twice divorced, and the British and Dominion governments would not consent to a marriage between her and the king. After he abdicated he became the Duke of Windsor and as his wife Mrs. Simpson became the Duchess of Windsor. |
| 1994 | Susie Evelyn "Dollie" Mann Noah died on December 26, 1994, at the Winona Manor Nursing Home in Winona, Mississippi. It had been twenty years since we had a death in the immediate family. |
| 1997 | Robert Randall Noah died on March 24, 1997, in the Tyler-Holmes Hospital in Winona, Mississippi. |

# Chapter 5   Early Life Journey

A. Introduction
B. Early Family Life
C. Early School Life
D. Early Religious Life

## A. Introduction

Spring time of my life
Carroll County, Mississippi
moments preserved

This is a story of a sentimental and simple time in my own history. The setting for those early years is Carroll County, Mississippi, one of the many rural parts of Mississippi, and, in fact, one of the most rural parts of the United States even today.

It was a place where modern America and the pace of change came slowly. It was a place I called home until I left for New Orleans in August 1956.

It was a place where we all spoke Southern, but had no awareness that others did not speak as we did. It was the place I was born and raised. It is a place I hold dear.

There are identified words and phrases that only Southerners or Southern transplants understand. Some of the most used ones include "ya'll," "pitch a hissie fit" or have a "conniption," "out yonder," "give me some sugar," give me a "Yankee dime," "make sweet eyes" or "sweet milk," "I'm fixin a mess of fish or a mess of turnip greens." If you don't know what these mean you will have to ask a P.R.I.T.S (Person Raised in the South.)

Times were not easy—we were a dirt farm family, and there was real labor involved just to put food on the table. We saw hard work in one way or another every day because a large part of our life revolved around just living—obtaining water from a well or cistern; growing, gathering, and preparing food; finding and chopping firewood; washing on a scrub board; ironing with heavy black irons; milking cows; chopping and picking cotton.

Even though farm life was labor intensive, we didn't seem as stressed as we are today. It is often said that we have more leisure time today than ever before, but it doesn't seem that way. During my early years out in the country of Carroll County and in the town of Vaiden, there were no telephones to chat with friends and family or to be harassed by someone trying to sell you something at the time you are the busiest. We weren't able to jump into an automobile to run an errand, we didn't have television, we didn't have potted houseplants, we didn't water our yard or garden, and we didn't mow or edge our lawn. We didn't have stopped up sinks, leaky commodes, bathrooms to clean, or carpets to vacuum.

We were poor—very poor, but we were never at the bottom rung of life, nor on the fringe of society. When we chopped and picked cotton, we did this after school or when school was out. One of the ways—when we were old enough to do the work—that we could make money was to chop and pick cotton. At Blackmonton we were hired by Mr. Bill Stuart and his son, John Lester, to pick their cotton. My brother Billy told me on May 25, 1996, that Daddy made at least one crop with Mr. Bill and John Lester. "We were laborers for Daddy and Mr. Bill and John Lester."

I recall that some of my school mates—specifically the Rufus Minyard Family—at the Blackmonton School were absent the first couple months of school in the fall. Their entire family was forced to go to the Mississippi Delta to pick cotton as a method of making money for the family. From time to time this family also moved north to Gary, Indiana, so that the mother and father could find work in the factories there. I always missed these friends when they were away.

A good part was that all of Mother's and Daddy's children were born healthy, mentally and physically. Our young life was fraught with hardships galore, but rather than giving in to those hardships, we took what was good and surged ahead. There were stones in our paths, but if others did not remove those stones, we cleared them for ourselves. It was not a forgone conclusion, but all of us took wings and flew away from farm life.

All of the country people lived in wood-frame unpainted houses with front porches. We had no electricity, running water, or telephone.

Electricity did come to our part of rural Mississippi when I was in the tenth grade. Prior to that, our nighttime our light came from coal oil lamps. My great uncle, John Ward Eades, delivered the coal oil to our house. It was stored in big drums, and from these drums we filled the lamps with the oil. Our family actually burned little of that coal oil since my dad believed in going to bed with the chickens and getting up at day break, a habit he maintained throughout his life in Carroll County.

Everyone cooked on a wood burning stove, and every house had a fireplace for wintertime heat. All families had piles of stove wood for the kitchen stove and a wood pile for the fireplace.

The wood used for the stove and the fireplace had to be collected from the woods. A tree was first cut down, and then sawed into logs. Sometimes the logs would be left whole to be place toward the back of the fireplace. Logically, it was called a back stick. Other logs were split into various size pieces to either fit the stove or the fireplace.

To build a fire in the stove or in the fireplace took a certain procedure. The stove wood and fireplace wood would not burn without kindling—little pieces of pine that easily ignited—or some paper wadded and soaked with coal oil—sometimes called kerosene—used as a starter. A match was then used to ignite the starter source. From the starter source the other wood would start to burn.

Many modern day fireplaces are built for folks who long nostalgically for past days. I never have longed for a fireplace. A big reason is that I recall a family tragedy associated with our fireplace at Blackmonton. In early January 1997, Bobby, my brother, and I sat and talked about the day he was burned when his clothes caught on fire while he was sitting in front of the fireplace. He was three or four years old. He gave me this account. "Mother was making the beds. She looked around, and saw that my britches were on fire. She tried to get them off, but couldn't. She ran across the hall to get a pair of scissors. She was able to cut them off." That is all that he could recall. I do recall that Sarah, Billy, and I arrived home from school and learned that Bobby had been burned. Several days later he was taken to the doctor, and the burn was much greater than my parents had realized. Later on he spent time in Grenada Hospital and had multiple skin grafts. He could not walk for a long time and would scoot around on his butt. We pulled him in a little wagon. I was sad thinking he would never walk again. But he did. He now walks fine but he has a scarred leg, though on occasions he does have pain in that leg. This traumatic experience—which could have been a handicap for him—has not hindered his success in life.

Our water either came from a cistern or a well. We had a pail of water some place either in the kitchen or hanging on the front porch. Everyone in the family and guests, too, drank water out of the same pail. Every one also used a common dipper. When my aunt, Verna Duke, visited with her daughter, Janice, she didn't allow Janice to drink out of the common dipper. We all thought that was very strange. Only later in life we learned my aunt's idea seemed sensible.

During the winter months and sometimes in the summer we took baths in what we called a wash pan—a small shallow pan—where we put water that was warmed in the fireplace or on the wood burning stove. Only in the summer we took baths—maybe once or twice a week—in a large galvanized tub. My sister and I got stark naked without worrying about closing doors. We bathed in the same tub of water and used the same towel.

Without electricity, there was no refrigeration. But in the summertime ice by the fifty or hundred pounds was delivered to us when *The Iceman Cometh* in a pick-up truck. We stored the ice in the hulls that we fed the cows. The ice lasted about one week, and then the ice man returned. The ice made it possible for us to have ice tea to drink in the summertime. We drank sweet tea, and I really didn't know people drank tea without sugar until much later in life.

At other times the ice was stored in something we called an icebox. The icebox was not electrical and it would not make ice, but it looked like a small modern day refrigerator. Apparently it was insulated, as the ice didn't melt as fast as it did sitting outside of the icebox.

All families had outdoor toilets or privies, as they were sometimes called. One of ours had a toilet with two seats. I guess we were supposed to alternate using them. It seems ridiculous, but my sister and I use to hide in the outdoor toilet when dishwashing time came around. Sarah and I also had a playhouse in the outdoor toilet at various times, though that too seems incomprehensible to me. But it did happen. In the wintertime when it was cold, we used an enamel slop jar—an enamel bucket with a top on it—that we brought indoors to use during the night and it would be emptied the next morning.

Because we had no telephones, we frequently went to see our neighbors, and they did not know we were coming. We were always welcome, and they were virtually assured to be at home. Most of them did not have automobiles. Because Mother liked to go visiting, we visited them many more times than they visited us. We went to see Miss Gladys, Miss Susie, Miss Lula, and Miss Lottie. They might be sitting on the porch or in a hallway shelling butter beans, snapping green beans, or shucking corn. But they would either stop and chat or continue what they were doing and chat anyway.

Other than at Miss Gladys's, we generally didn't go inside the house, and the visits were short. Miss Gladys's house was the cleanest house I was ever in, then or now. She had chickens on the yard and she even picked up the chicken feathers. She was a smoker, and when she sat down to smoke, she had a wet dishcloth in her hand to clean up the ashes in the event an ash or two missed the ashtray. In my youth I thought that was great and that everyone should be as meticulous as Miss Gladys was about cleanliness.

When we visited, we weren't served any refreshments, nor did we expect any. It was a time of pleasant relaxation and never do I remember the word stress ever being used. That early experience of visiting neighbors without calling is something I still enjoy. I love for friends to stop by without prior notice if they are passing my house.

My family never owned a car. Out of necessity, we either walked or rode a horse. Horse riding was not for sport or diversion. I knew how to ride a horse from childhood. We would go out into the pasture and jump upon the horse bareback or lead the horse by the head to the barn, put the saddle on, and then ride. Sometimes we did bum rides with other people into town—this meant to the small town of Vaiden—and to church.

Lera Pinkston, a family friend, told a story at the time of Mother's funeral, December 29, 1994, about Mother's resourcefulness in getting to Enon to see her family. "Dollie would get a ride to Enon with the mailman to see Mr. Floyd and Miss Maggie."

In my own memory bank, I recall that we sometimes rode in a wagon to Enon. All of this proves if there is a will, there is a way.

We did have vehicular transportation to school. My early school bus was not the big yellow one, but a pick-up truck that had a covered bed on it. Through rain or shine, that school bus was there for us. By the time we started to Vaiden School, we did have a big yellow school bus. Bad weather did not inhibit our school bus from arriving in a timely manner.

I have no recall of any school bus problems. We never had a flat tire, got stuck in the mud, or had any other bus problem.

The one lane country roads of red clay or medium dark brown sand that got muddy with a rain were always a worry when it rained for those persons with cars and trucks. From experience they knew they might literally get "stuck in the mud" or drive into a ditch. It would have been risky business to drive without tire chains, especially in the wintertime. Deep muddy ruts—if one suggests that they are in a rut this comes to my mind—were created when a car or truck drove in the mud. The next person coming along would have to stay in the same rut.

Upkeep of these roads was the job of the beat supervisor who had an elected position. My grandfather ran for this political job on at least two occasions but was not elected. The supervisor—really one of the folks working under him—had this big machinery which was used to grade the roads and get the ruts out. Folks commented—sometimes complained—about the condition of the roads and whether the supervisor was doing a good job with the road upkeep.

Later on the dirt roads were covered with gravel, which helped prevent the muddy ruts. There were bridges that had no rails over creeks. Many of those bridges remain without rails in this modern day. If two vehicles coming from different directions arrived at a bridge at the same time, one would have to wait for the other to cross. It was never a big problem since the traffic was very light.

Every family had a large vegetable garden. In the spring we had lots of turnip and mustard greens—vegetables that could be planted early and were prolific. In the fall we had green tomatoes for frying. In between we had many types of vegetables like eggplant, green beans, English peas, cucumbers, squash, okra, and many more.

Almost all of the vegetables were grown from seeds in well-prepared soil that was fertilized with barnyard fertilizer mixed in with the soil. Other loving care included keeping the garden free of weeds. After the garden grew, we had fresh vegetables to eat every day at lunchtime. Mother would go to the garden in the morning to gather and cook the vegetables by lunchtime. At night we ate leftovers or milk with cornbread in it.

Lots of vegetables were canned for wintertime eating. Mother either used a canner or a pressure cooker to prepare the vegetables for storage for the winter. Both the canner and the steam pressure cooker held approximately six quart jars. Using the pressure cooker could be tricky.

The vegetables would be gathered, washed, and prepared for cooking. They would be blanched on top of the stove and then put into quart jars and placed into the pressure cooker, which was placed on top of the stove to get hot. A gauge on top of the cooker would begin to rattle and you would then know that you had it at the correct temperature. You let that go on for a period of time and then remove the cooker from the heat. Here's what got tricky. All of the steam had to be out of the cooker before opening the top. Otherwise you could open it and the jars could break and vegetables would fly.

It was a simple time for clothing. Daddy always wore overalls for work and he didn't have many other clothes. He rarely wore a suit, but he always knew how to tie a necktie. He had one pair of high top shoes and maybe one more pair of shoes. Mother mostly wore homemade dresses, and she did have some that she wore around home every day and different clothes that she wore when she left home. On a rare occasion she would get to order a ready made dress from what we called the Roebuck—Sears now—or Montgomery Ward catalog. We called these catalogs "wish books."

Daddy, like all men, had a hat which he wore most of the time outside of the house. When they went to town and walked down the street, the men would tip their hats at a person they would meet. Men took their hats off in church. Women, too, wore hats to church, especially on Easter Sunday and to the Enon "dinner on the ground event."

We children didn't have many clothes. However, we did have different clothes that we wore to school, every day at home, and sometimes clothes that we only wore to church. We didn't wear blue jeans and Daddy didn't like for his girls to wear shorts that were worn above our knees. I was in the ninth grade before I had a pair of blue jeans, and they were made especially for girls with the opening on the side.

Generally, we had one pair of white sandals for the summer and another pair of brown or saddle oxford shoes for the winter season. We went barefoot when we were home in the summer and, in fact, that was something we looked forward to when school was out. We knew it was time to pull off our shoes and we could go barefoot until school started in the fall. But we always wore shoes to church and to school.

We had one clock that stayed on the mantle. Mother and Daddy and I, likewise, had a built-in biological clock, or it may have been either the crowing rooster or perhaps the sun. We never had an alarm clock, and none of us owned a wrist watch. That biological clock was more reliable and constant than the clock that set on the mantle.

That clock had to be hand wound. It went tick-tock day and night. On the hour the clock would strike the number of times that indicated the time of day it was. It struck twelve times at noon and at midnight.

One way we stayed current with the outside world was through the weekly newspaper appropriately named *The Conservative*. It helped us to stay current about who visited whom, who got married, and who died.

We also had a radio with tubes in it. I do not remember hearing news reports on the radio, but we did get the "Grand Ole Opry" from Nashville, Tennessee. Minnie Pearl I remember was on the, "Grand Ole Opry," and her unforgettable voice saying something like this: "Howdy. Don't forget the Americanaise Coffee." From the "Grand Ole Opry" and from the country music heard throughout the week, I listened to and learned to love country music. The lyrics were often sad, but the beat was great. One unforgettable tune was "The Tennessee Waltz." Also on the radio we heard Sam Morris, a radio evangelist from Del Rio, Texas.

Our mail was delivered by a mail carrier who drove his own pick-up truck. We had a mail-box about a half mile from our house for him to leave the mail. If we had mail to send we would raise a little flag on the mail box so the mail carrier would know to pick it up. A post card was sent for one cent and a letter for three cents.

Besides visiting our neighbors, other social events were school and church activities. On a few occasions we went to a traveling carnival that was going on in Vaiden.

A big church event was not a wedding, but a church funeral. No one was buried without a church funeral. When a person died, most of the community shared in the family's sorrow. On one occasion—the funeral of Mrs. Lula Stuart—school was dismissed and most of the school children attended the funeral.

People died at home. A doctor had to be contacted to come to pronounce the person dead. The funeral home would come to pick up the body. After the person was embalmed by the funeral home, the body would be returned home in a casket to lie in state for a few days and nights. A dead person was never left alone once the body was returned home. Even at night there were people, at least two, who stayed in the room with the deceased. It was called "setting up."

Then and now neighbors, friends, and church members brought loads of food to the deceased's family's home. Besides being a big social event for the community, it was a way of seeing lots of relatives who came from far and near. My recall is that black folks usually kept the deceased's body in the home a lot longer than white folks. They had to wait for the relatives to come from places like Chicago and Detroit, and all of them got there one way or another.

## B. Family Life

A chronicle of my early life is a story like many others. Knowing this, I invite you on a journey of my early life in Mississippi. Read along for the thorns and roses.

I—Carolyn Sue Noah—was home-delivered by Dr. M. E. Arrington on December 29, 1938, at 11: 30 p.m. in the Blackmonton Community—too tiny for a map to show—of Carroll County, Mississippi. Franklin Delano Roosevelt was in his second term as president of the United States. He was re-elected in 1940 and in 1944 for an unprecedented fourth term.

My parents were Robert Randall and Susie Evelyn "Dollie" Mann Noah. I was their first child, my paternal grandparents' first grandchild, and the first child of a daughter of my maternal grandparents. That birthday went without a celebration until I was married and my mother-in-law began to make it special. She, too, was a December child. My astrological sign is Capricorn.

Mother breast-fed me, as well as her other four children. I followed that tradition with my own children, though it was uncommon to breast feed with my generation at that time. According to Mother, I was a healthy baby until at the age of six weeks I had pneumonia. Mother told me that I almost died. That must have been the first battle of my life. That battle won, I have never had any respiratory problem since other than what is commonly referred to as a "head cold" and occasional tonsillitis.

When I asked my mother where my name came from, she told me from a radio program, "Sue and Lou the Tucker Twins." When my sister came along three years later her middle name was Lou. Growing up, I was generally called Sue except one aunt—Daddy's brother's wife, Louise Eades Noah—called me Carolyn Sue.

Carroll County was my home until I was seventeen. The first fourteen of those seventeen years were spent in the country approximately ten miles outside of the small town of Vaiden, Mississippi.

## The Weaning House

At the time of my birth, my parents lived across the hollow—that's how we described the location—from Daddy's parents. The house was a two room wood frame, with just a bedroom and a kitchen. It was unpainted except for white wash on the wall of the front porch. (White wash was a mixture of water and white clay collected from the area around the Old Salem Community.) The roof of the house was tin and the floors were wide wood planks. There were no rugs or even linoleum over the bare floors. There was a barbed wire fence across the front of the house to keep the cows from getting out, and there was an outdoor toilet.

In the late nineteen nineties, my Aunt Louise Eades Noah, told me this was called the "weaning house." This little house had served as the first home for Mother and Daddy when they moved from my paternal grandparents' home and later for my Uncle Ken and Aunt Louise when they moved from Ken's parents' home.

I feel sure I was born in this house as I know Mother's aunt—we called her Cedy—came to help Mother when I was born. Cedy, never married and childless, "had her own way of doing things." One long ago story that I heard was that her way and my dad's way did not make for a congenial interaction during my early babyhood. For instance, she believed that an adult should chew the baby's food and then feed it to the baby.

My earliest memory is a glimpse of an accident that I had when Mother and Daddy and I lived in this little house across the hollow. I was not yet three. I can hear Mother yelling for help. In my vague memory I can hear Mother saying that Papa Randall, my great—grandfather, heard her and came over to the house. I had fallen off the porch, and there was a large gash in my head between my eyebrows. The evidence goes with me today in the scar that I have between my eyebrows.

We were still living in that little house across the hollow from my grandparents when my sister, Sarah Lou, was born. However, Mother was at the home of her parents in the Enon Community of Carroll County when Dr. Arrington home-delivered Sarah at 1:58 A.M.—she was born a night owl—on December 1, 1941. On December 7, 1941, when she was seven days old, Pearl Harbor was bombed.

## The John Lee House

According to Dell Lee, Daddy's first cousin, our family of four moved to what was called the John Lee Place in January 1942. From that day forward we called it the John Lee House. It was on the property of my great-grandfather and named for his son-in-law, John Lee. I ask today why wasn't it wasn't called the Minnie Lee Place since she was his daughter.

Another of his daughters Mae and her husband, John Boone, also lived on his property, and their home was called the John Boone place. He must have liked his sons-in-law.

Our house on the John Lee Place was low on the ground, and I wonder why, as most houses were built up to prevent flooding. It was an unpainted wood frame house with a rusty tin roof.

I remember there was a barn behind the house, and there was a cow pen nearby. A memory—either heard or witnessed—that I have is that Mother got upset with Daddy one time when they were milking cows, and she threw a milk bucket at him. From that day forward, I have no recall that either of them used any kind of physical violence toward each other. But they perfected the art of yelling and screaming at each other.

Our closest neighbors were black families. One family was Sarah and Andrew Meeks and their grandchildren. Andrew looked like Jack Spratt and Sarah looked like the wife who could eat no lean. Other black families were the Sam and Molly Griffin family, and the "Snat" Griffin family.

I think they all lived on the property of my great-grandfather. We were close to them in distance and in spirit. That spirit only went so far. The Black folks came in the back door, called my father, Mr. Robert and my mother, Miss Dollie, and would eventually begin to call me Miss Sue. Abraham Lincoln's Emancipation on September 22, 1861 had done nothing to change this.

The grandchildren of Sarah and Andrew, Martha Sue and W. L, were my first playmates. We played by the hour under what we called black jack oak trees. They didn't know they weren't white and I didn't know I wasn't black. It didn't matter, we were children and having playmates was all that was important.

In Mississippi where I grew up, we children also called the folks older than we were Miss Susie, Miss Gladys, Miss Lottie, Miss Helen whether they were married or single. My early school teachers were addressed in this same manner. We also were taught to say "yes, ma'am" and "no, ma'am" and "yes, sir" and "no, sir." Mother didn't like "yeah and naw." Though Mother was not always successful in getting that across to her children when we answered her, we did honor senior members in our lives with "yes, ma'am", "no, ma'am" or "yes, sir "and "no, sir." In later life I dropped the ma'am and just used yes and no.

## The Heggie Place

By September 1944 our family had moved to the Heggie Place, a place owned by Daddy's uncle, Mood "Big Bud" Randall. We had a Coila, Mississippi, address. The house, a wood frame, unpainted house with a tin roof, was high off the ground. It had five rooms which included two bedrooms, a kitchen, a dining room, and a front room, called living room today. This house is still standing. All of the other houses that I lived in during my Mississippi years have either been torn down or fallen down.

The front room of this house was sometimes used for country dances. Music for the dances was provided by a guitarist and a fiddler. Mr. Oscar Coleman often played the guitar and Miss Susie Stuart played the fiddle.

Dell Lee, Daddy's first cousin, told me after Mother's funeral in 1994 that Mother gave him his first dancing lesson when he was a teenager. "I was trying to do a two step and Dollie told me it was a rag."

Dell also told me that the dancing arrangements would often be made late on Saturday afternoon. "We would then ride a horse around the country side to notify folks of the Saturday night dance."

My oldest brother, Billy Layne, was home-delivered by Dr. Arrington at Heggie Place on September 18, 1944, at 11:10 a.m. One of my early memories of him is an early birthday; he must have been one or two years old, celebration with him eating angel food cake. Another early memory of him is a photograph with him wearing cowboy boots and hat that our Uncle Percy Mann sent him from Montana.

Our closest neighbors at the Heggie place were black folks, Skeet Williams, John and Louisa Haslip, and the Bob Boles Family. One Christmas John Haslip was at our house, and he and I climbed up into the attic—we called it the loft—for some unremembered reason. But the attic floor was not strong and we both fell to the floor.

Our white neighbors lived farther away. The Schumachers' house was the only house that I remember was actually painted instead of white washed. Other white neighbors were the Pinkstons, my dad's great-Uncle Luther, Luther's son Clyde with his wife and children, the L. C. Hodges Family, and the Oscar Coleman family. The Coleman's had two girls who were about my age—Jeanette and Shirley. We often played together. I recall that we were at their house more than they were at ours. Sometimes Mother nagged Sarah and me for staying at their house too long.

They were all family friends, but we seemed to have had more interaction with the Pinkstons. Miss Blanche Pinkston was a widow and many of her children had grown up and left home. Miss Blanche was especially afraid of a black cloud and always had a storm pit that she went to often. Miss Blanche didn't lose her life to a storm, but died in a car wreck.

Miss Blanche's youngest daughter, Marguerite loved to dance, and I remember her coming to our house and begging Mother to have a dance. Mother accommodated Marguerite from time to time. In later years Marguerite and some of her siblings became Pentecostal Church members, and their beliefs did not allow dancing, make-up or cutting their hair. I never attended a Pentecostal Church, but the rumor was that they would throw their children up in the air they would get so happy, and sometimes the adults would pass out.

My most vivid memories of Santa Claus are from the Heggie Place. We put out cookies and milk, and after Santa Claus came, Daddy would wake us up to let us know that Santa Claus had come and gone. Knowing that Daddy would wake us up filled us with anticipation. It was one of Daddy's joys, but Mother didn't particularly like it. After we were awakened, Sarah and I would get up and play with our new toys until we fell asleep once again.

Mother was probably too tired from cooking, cleaning, and getting everything in order for Christmas Day to appreciate the fun we were having. She would usually bake at least two cakes, a fruitcake and a coconut cake. There were no cake mixes, and the coconut was a real one that you had to break open with a hammer, pick out the pieces, and then shred. It was good but lots of work. Mother did all of this cooking on a wood burning stove. She also had three children under the age of ten.

**Billy Noah
wearing Cowboy Hat**

**Billy Noah in U.S.Air Force**

My other memories of the Heggie Place are many and varied. Most of our food came from a vegetable garden. The cows provided milk and butter, along with pigs, chickens, and sometimes quail were our source of meat. Chickens also provided eggs. One time we had a pig that we fed at the back door every day. It became a pet, but at hog killing time it was killed for its meat. Daddy liked to hunt for quail and we would pick, clean, cook, and eat the birds that he killed.

We picked wild blackberries and scuppernongs, also called muscadines, for jams and jellies in the woods. As we picked the berries and scuppernongs, we placed them in tin one-gallon molasses buckets. While picking the berries redbugs—little insects that flourish in the woods—got on us. They especially liked to get under our arms and bury themselves. This would cause you to itch and itch until they were removed.

At the Heggie Place our water came from a well just as it had at the John Lee Place. We still used a galvanized tub for bathing.

In the wintertime we took a bath—using what we called a wash pan—with water that was heated in a black iron kettle on the stove or at the fireplace. In the summer we often took a tub bath using a large galvanized tub. Several of us bathed in the same tub of water.

My greatest recall of the well has to do with washing day. Mother drew enough water from the well for three tubs and a big black pot. The black pot had a fire under it, and the clothes that were hard to clean were boiled in that pot to get some of the dirt out. Daddy wore these heavy denim overalls to work in and they got especially dirty, and were always boiled in the pots.

There were either two or three galvanized tubs of water. The first washing tub had warm water that was heated in the black wash pot and a scrub board. You scrubbed the clothes on the board with a large bar of soap. You started the wash with the white clothes and gradually scrubbed all of the clothes. After getting the dirt out of the clothes, you wrung them out and placed them into the next tub, which often had bluing in it to make the white clothes whiter. Most of the time there was another tub to rinse the clothes again.

After the final rinsing and wringing, the clothes were placed in a pail for hanging on the line. We hung the clothes on a barbed wire fence to dry and hoped it would be a rain-free day.

All of the clothing was made mostly of cotton, and anything you wore on the outside had to be ironed. Many of the clothes were starched and had to be hand-sprinkled prior to ironing. Ironing was another day's work in which the heavy black irons were heated either on the wood burning stove or an outside fire. In the wintertime, the irons were heated in the fireplace. Many times when ironing something light colored, you got smut—a particle of soot—on them and they had to be washed again.

Our pet dog, Doolittle, named for General Doolittle of World War II fame, was the only real pet other than the little pig written about earlier. But Daddy did have other dogs for quail hunting. Doolittle became sick, and had what we called fits. During these fits the dog went around in circles as if it were chasing its tail, and out of its mouth came this frothy foam. When it had the fits, Mother would grab the broom, we would all get upon the bed, and Mother fought the dog off until the fit was over. Mother called it a mad dog, and while it seems impossible to believe, Mother said it had hydrophobia. We didn't kill it nor have it put to sleep. It just died. We were lucky that no one got bitten.

We lived at the Heggie Place long enough for Mother to have a fourth child, her second son, Robert Mann "Bobby." Bobby was born on March 4, 1947, at 12:25 a.m. in Vaiden, Mississippi.

He was born at the home of Ken and Louise Noah, Daddy's brother and sister-in-law. Mother's doctor was Dr. Burnham. Louise gave a personal account of helping with Bobby's birth. "Dr. Burnham told me to observe for umbilical cord bleeding. However, I was very tired, went to sleep, and woke up the next morning to find the cord encrusted in old blood. I called the doctor right away, but there was no problem. It was merely old blood."

He was given the name Robert Mann Noah, but growing up he had various nicknames. We called him "Baby Brother," "Bae," "Bobby," and our Mann cousins called him "Robbie" for a long time. The "Baby Brother" did not stick as he was usurped from that position when our next brother was born. On July 4, 1997 Bobby told me that he was also called "Nigger Boy" by our dad. Bobby said that he and Daddy would go up town, and when Daddy was ready to go home he would yell out loud so folks in town could hear him. "Let's go Nigger Boy." He would know to catch up with Daddy, knowing it was time to go home.

While Mother was in Vaiden giving birth and recuperating, Sarah, Billy, and I stayed with our great uncle, Turner Mann, and his wife Lola. Turner was our grandfather Floyd's baby brother. We have remained close to that family from that day forward.

During our visit with our great-uncle Uncle Turner and Aunt Lola, my two and one-half-year-old brother, Billy provided some entertainment singing "Bingle Bells" at the kitchen table. He was probably encouraged to perform, but why "Bingle Bells, Bingle all the way" in March, I have no explanation.

Another short story about our stay there has to do with me. I think I was coughing and Aunt Lola wanted to give me an aspirin. I was eight years old but I never remembered taking any kind of medicine, other than the castor oil I mentioned before, and I did not want to take it. I think I was strongly encouraged and finally did agree.

When Mother and our new baby brother were ready to come home, R.P. Day drove us home. R.P. was the husband of my grandfather's first cousin, Mary Noah Day. They were family but also good friends. A rather vivid memory of mine about our arrival home is that R. P. picked Mother up and carried her up the rickety steps. Mother now had four children, all less than ten years of age, and a husband who needed her care. I was eight, my sister was five, Billy was two and one-half, and now she had an infant. Being a homemaker was not an easy job and the pay was not good either.

**Bobby Noah**

**Bobby Noah**

On July 4th of that same year Mother's brother, Victor Mann, accidentally fell from his son-in-law's truck and was badly injured. He died shortly after the accident. This early loss of life was terrible, and was even worse since Victor's wife, Vera, had died only three years earlier and left him with six young children.

One daughter, Martha, was married. The other five children—Dorothy, Virginia, Bubber, Bobbie Ann, and Hayden—were still living at home. I was told by Martha and Dorothy in May of 2000 that it was suggested that the children would have to go to an orphanage, but this didn't happen.

## Our Grandparents' House

In 1948 or 1949 our family of six moved back into the house of my dad's parents. My parents had made a circle in that they lived with them when they first got married. I am not sure why the move was made. My grandparents may have thought they would get my father out of the bootleg whiskey making with his great Uncle Luther. It wouldn't have been as convenient since at the Heggie Place we lived within a mile of Uncle Luther and my grandparents home may have been three miles. That's not a lot of difference except that Daddy had no convenient transportation. It is likely that he participated less in the production process of bootleg whiskey, but he still had no problem finding it to drink, plus he had the skill to make home brew.

Our move into my grandparents' home was followed by a move into the town of Vaiden by my grandparents and their baby daughter, Ruth. I asked my Aunt Ruth, Daddy's sister, on July 19, 1993, sitting in a Grenada Hospital room when Daddy was in the operating room for a broken hip repair, why they had moved into town. Her response, "I reckon it was because they were getting old." My grandfather was sixty-two or sixty-three and my grandmother was either fifty-five or fifty-six, both younger than I am as I write this book. But I feel young and seem younger than I felt they were at the time.

This house was built for my grandparents and their children. It was a wood frame, unpainted house with white wash on the walls of the front porch. It was built high off the ground upon sand rocks, and to get into the house you had to go up eight or so wooden steps in front of the house that took you onto the front porch. The house had five rooms with a large hall separating one side of the house from the other. The hall was a large enclosed area which served as a work area and a sitting area. There we spent time shelling butterbeans and peas and stringing beans. If we had company we sat there or on the front porch.

The kitchen was separate from the rest of the house, but there was a little catwalk you passed through to get into the kitchen. A screened back porch was attached to the kitchen. A cellar for preserving the canned vegetables in glass jars was located under the house.

There were no closets. One of the bedrooms—we called it the "backroom or side room"—had a clothes line wire across the back which we used to hang the clothes that were not folded. Later on Mother bought a chifforobe—piece of furniture similar to an armoire, but smaller—where we hung clothes on one side and used drawers on the other side for folded clothes. A floor length mirror was on the clothes hanging side that let us look at ourselves from head to toe. It was particularly useful for observing the hemline of a dress or skirt.

Sarah and I slept in this little side room most of the time. But in the wintertime because of the cold I think all of us slept in the room with the fireplace. However, there was no fire after we went to bed. Daddy got up and built a fire the next morning. We had feather beds and used a warm brick wrapped in paper to keep our feet warm at night.

Some of the rooms had wallpaper on them, but otherwise the walls were bare or white washed. The kitchen was especially dark, almost black, due to the smoke from the wood stove.

A large porch—my grandfather, Tom called it a gallery—extended across the entire width of the house. A wooden water bucket hung from the ceiling on the north side of the porch. A wisteria vine covered the south side. It provided shade in the summer, and in the winter it was bare to let the sun in. In the middle of the porch we had a porch swing. The swing served a wonderful purpose and we used it by the hour.

The front yard had some wild grass, but since we freely walked on it grass cutting was not necessary, so our farm tools did not include a lawn mower. On each side of the front door steps, cannas grew. In one corner of the yard there was a deep pink crepe myrtle, and on the other side there were a couple of roses.

My entry into the world of flower gardening began in this front yard. I dug up some of the grass in front of the cannas and planted a row of zinnias. Those zinnias really performed and thus I received my reward.

That reward gave momentum to my love of flower gardening from that day forward.

Just outside the barbed wire backyard fence we had our outdoor toilet. It had two seats—that was a luxury, I guess—but other than when my sister and I made a playhouse or hid from Mother to escape from washing the dishes, we used the facility alone. It was a chilly place in the winter, and yes, we did use the Sears catalog for toilet paper, but at the time we called it the Roebuck catalog. We never seemed to run out of paper, and certainly our use of the Roebuck catalog was recycling at its optimum. At night time we would sometimes use what we called a slop jar.

There were several barns. None were red. One was an old unused one, another newer barn had a cow pen, and a smaller barn-like structure, where we kept meal and hulls made from cottonseed to feed the cows. Other outside buildings included a henhouse and a little house for fattening pigs to kill.

There were two ponds. The cows drank out of them and peed in them, and we played in those same ponds. We never heard of any reason not to do so. Public health was not an issue, and we were never sick from the muddy bacteria-laden water.

We had a storm pit as a haven for bad weather. Mother was deathly afraid of tornados. (We called them storms.) This storm pit was dug into the side of a little hill. The top was covered with logs and then a heaping mound of dirt. We had no radio or television for weather reports; therefore, acting as her own weather person, Mother went by the black clouds in the sky, the thunder and lightning, and it was her call. Daddy never went with us, and never seemed a bit concerned about the weather.

Fear of the tornados was not an unreasonable fear in that we knew of one family tragedy in which two members of the John Tom Walker family were killed during a tornado. That was a sad occasion and gave cause for fear and alarm when the weather was bad.

To go to the storm pit was spooky, but fun. We would all be huddled together with a lantern to provide light. Though it may have rained hard, and there was thunder and lightning, we never experienced a tornado, no lives were lost other than the little pet billy goat that we had when the chain around its neck that was struck by lightning. Losing that pet billy goat was sad, but it had gotten too wild to allow it to run loose.

Mother cooked two or three meals every day. The entire family always ate together. Mother sometimes blessed the food. Daddy didn't pray, but he never allowed giggling at the table. If we got tickled over something, we knew to leave the table.

Every morning Mother made homemade biscuits. For dinner—we called our noon meal dinner—Mother either gathered fresh vegetables from the garden that same morning or we had home canned vegetables from what we called fruit jars from the cellar, or on rare occasions store bought canned vegetables. For supper—our night meal—we ate leftovers or had a glass of milk with bread.

Out on the farm we were basically self-sufficient when it came to food. We had a large vegetable garden, a pecan orchard, an apple orchard, and we gathered wild blackberries, plums, and muscadines for jellies, jams and berry pies.

Mother canned vegetables to have to eat during the winter months, and these vegetables were placed in a cellar under the house. We had an apple orchard. Every apple tree was different. We even had a yellow delicious apple tree. Some of the apples were made into jellies and some were dried for future eating just as they were or for use in apple pies. My sister and I climbed by ladder or an old plank to place some of the apples that had been cut up on top of the small barn to dry.

We grew our own chickens for meat and for eggs. We grew pigs into hogs for other meat and for lard to use for cooking. We had molasses made out of sorghum cane and milked the cows for milk and butter for our own use and to sell.

Our chicken supply came from chickens we raised from baby chicks. Hens laid eggs that were either eaten, used for cooking cakes, pies, and cornbread and other food when the recipe called for eggs.

Sometimes a hen stayed on the nest, and we knew that she was ready to incubate eggs. We called her a "setting hen." Some of the eggs were placed in the nest under her for a period of incubation. Hens stayed on the nest approximately three weeks, leaving the nest infrequently. After the incubation time, the eggs began to crack and eventually little chicks were born. For a period of time those little chicks followed the mother hen and ate what they could find on the ground if they were not otherwise fed.

Regularly we had fried chicken from our own stock. Mother caught the chicken from the yard or took it out of the brooder. The method that Mother used to kill the chickens seems rather brutal to me today. After catching the chicken, she took it by the neck and literally wrung its head off. The head stayed in her hand and the rest of the chicken fell to the ground. The other method used to kill the chicken was no less brutal. Sometimes Mother tied the chicken to the clothesline, and just cut its head off with a knife. This part of farm life I was only a spectator. After this brutal—at least, by my modern thinking—death, Mother placed the chicken into hot water to loosen the feathers. The feathers were plucked, the chicken's guts were removed, and finally the chicken was cut into pieces for frying.

Some of the young hens and one rooster—that rooster had a harem—were let free to roam the yard. The chicken cycle began all over. Hens laid the eggs in the henhouse that were fertilized by roosters; hens sat on the eggs to incubate them; little baby chickens—we called them deedies—were hatched, placed in the brooder to grow to a size for eating or given their freedom to wander the yard.

Another source of meat was cholesterol-laden hogs. A sow gave birth to little pigs. She nursed them until they were old enough to eat the slop—a mixture of water with everything left over from our family meals—or corn, which could be shelled or fed to the pigs on the cob. One or two of the pigs were placed in a special hog pen to be force fed with a lot of corn.

On a cold winter day the fattened hog lost its life on "hog killing day." Hog killing day was a kind of ritual, often a small community event in which neighbors assisted neighbors. The hog would be killed with a shotgun, dipped in hot water to loosen the hair, and then hung from a tree limb to be cut up into various pieces of meat—ham, bacon, and short ribs. The hams cured in the smokehouse using salt lasted for months if not a year.

None of the hog was wasted. Most country people would eat any part of the hog including the liver; the stomach called tripe; the pancreas; the tongue; and even the hog guts. Chitling—guts of the hog—suppers were one of the social events associated with hog killing. It was one event that I skipped, but I smelled the chitlings cooking the entire day.

Some meat was ground for sausage. On the night of the hog killing and the next morning, we had sausage patties and homemade biscuits. We had eggs mixed with the hog's brain, and the fat and grisly feet were cooked on hot coals in the fireplace to eat.

The skin of the hog was boiled in the heavy black iron pot we used for heating water for washing clothes. The resulting boiled cracklings produced our lard. At first the lard was a thick liquid. It solidified. This lard and the ham bones were used to season our turnip

At Blackmonton I have my most memorable experiences with regards to milking cows. I especially remember Daddy and me getting up before sunrise around 4:30 a.m. to milk the cows and put the milk on the road for the milkman by 6 a.m. Daddy never owned an alarm clock and never wore a watch, but he always got up on time, awakened me, and left to pick up the milk can from the road.

Often times I got up right away and swept the back yard where the geese had slept the night before and left their droppings. Mother hated to get up and see the geese droppings, and one way to keep her happy was for me to sweep before she was up to cook breakfast. Other mornings I would wait for Daddy to call me when he got back from the road with the milk can, but I was always ready to move when he came back for me. We walked to the cow pen together, father and daughter. When a farm man has a daughter as the first born, that daughter learns to adapt to the expectations.

Daddy and I hand milked several cows, and then strained the milk into a milk can to take to the road for the milkman to pick up. The person milking sat on a stool facing the cow at the cow's right side toward the back by the tits. The milk bucket was placed under the tits. You grabbed the tits, often two at a time, and squeezed the milk into the bucket until no more milk was left in that tit. You took all of her milk, and she usually had all day to make more.

We saved some of the milk for family use. Our milk for personal use was neither pasteurized nor homogenized. Neither was it refrigerated. Generally, we did not drink the milk right away, but morning milk was drunk at night. Just for fun we might squeeze some of the milk directly from the cow into our mouths or maybe into the mouth of a little brother.

Some milk was allowed to sour and later churned for butter. After scooping the butter off the top, we had buttermilk to drink or to make cornbread and biscuits.

Sometimes after milking the cows I went back to bed. Mother frowned upon this practice, but I did it anyway, and over the years I have become accustomed to having fun made about my sleeping habits. I have not outgrown my need for seven to eight hours of sleep every night and sometimes a short nap feels good in between.

After milking, the cows were let out to graze during the day. In the late afternoon, my sister Sarah and I and sometimes my oldest brother Billy who would have been only seven or eight years old, were in charge of finding the cows and herding them into the cow pen for the night. The pasture was large, and sometimes you didn't know which direction they went to graze during the day. One cow wore a cowbell, and that helped us to locate the herd. Sometimes we walked and at other times we rode a horse to get the cows.

In the wintertime the cows did not have much grass to graze so they were fed hulls, made from cottonseed, and cottonseed meal in troughs. During those cold winter months, the cows slept inside the barn.

Sometimes Sarah and Billy did some milking, but my recall of their helping with this chore is not great. On March 11, 2000, my brother Billy and I talked about milking cows. He even recalled some of the names of the cows including Ed, Belhaven, and Brooks.

The few groceries we bought usually came from the country store. We bought such items as flour, salt, soap, and a few other staples. Mr. Sam Clements owned the store. Mr. Clements was a bachelor, and he lived in the back of the store. His bachelor quarters were small and much like bachelor quarters of today except he had an outdoor toilet.

This store was about two miles away. If you had asked me at the time I would probably have said ten. We either walked or rode a horse. One of the horses that we rode was Dixie. On March 11, 2000, my brother, Billy told me that Dixie's mother was named Black and perhaps we had ridden Black to the store before Dixie.

We had a running account in which we charged our groceries throughout the month. When our monthly milk check came, we paid Mr. Clements. I remember we would not spend more than twenty dollars for the entire month. We occasionally had enough change left over to buy a soft drink, and many times that drink was an RC/Royal Crown Cola. Sometimes we would also be able to get a Milky Way or Butterfinger.

Our light, except the sunlight, moonlight and the stars, came from coal oil lamps until around 1953, when we got electricity out in the country. We went to bed with the chickens, an idea of Daddy's to save the oil and to make it easy for us to get up at the break of day. We used that God-given light to its best advantage.

I was in the tenth grade when country living changed for us a bit. Electricity arrived out in the rural parts of Mississippi. At first we had only the electric lights. These lights hung on a long cord hanging from the ceiling. We never had any table lamps.

Our first electrical appliance was a wringer washing machine, and this changed our washday activities, a little, but we still had to draw the water out of the cistern and pour it into the washing machine and the galvanized washtubs. But we didn't have to scrub the clothes on the scrub board, and the two rollers on the machine were used to wring the clothes out. Our clothes were still hung on a line to dry.

Other conveniences came with the electricity, such as an electric iron, and when our grandparents moved into our house, they brought their electric refrigerator with them. To this day I have a great appreciation for the automatic washing machine and dryer. I rarely plug in an electric iron without my childhood memory of the black iron that caused smut on clothes coming to the surface.

We lived in a county with lots of farming where the children were farm hands. Therefore, we had only eight months of school, September through April. We helped to chop cotton in the spring and pick cotton in the fall.

Daddy worked the fields with a mule and a plow. Each cotton row, each row of corn, and each garden row—man and animal with a plow—went up and down each of them. As directions, Daddy told the animal to gee or haw. The animal knew that gee meant to turn right and that haw meant to turn left.

Daddy planted cotton. He had to borrow money from the Holmes County Bank in Vaiden for the seeds. He then had to return to the bank for a loan for the fertilizer and the poison used to prevent the boll weevils from eating the cotton bolls. By the time he paid his debts, there was little if any money left over for the family.

Cotton was planted in the early spring, and when we got out of school, it was time for cotton chopping. The first chopping was to thin the cotton so that the stalks would not compete with each other for the food in the ground. We were back in the fields with hoes in the summer to rid the cotton of the competing weeds.

The cotton stalks grew often higher than five feet. They produced hibiscus type bloom, and the fruit of this bloom was a boll which held the cotton with the seeds. At first the boll was like a hard green ball, later it turned brown and popped open with fluffy white cotton. It was now ready for picking by human hand pickers.

The job of cotton picking was serious, but never stressful or frenetic. When there was a large group, especially if the cotton pickers included black folks, we talked, sang, and did lots of laughing. We wore old clothes and usually wore a hat to protect us from the sun. It never occurred to us that one day sunbathing and getting a suntan would become a popular thing to do. But we didn't know about the Mississippi and Florida beaches then.

We picked cotton after school and all day on Saturdays, but never on a Sunday. Daddy picked cotton, my sister, Sarah picked cotton, and I picked cotton. Later my brother, Billy, picked cotton. I will die with the hands of a cotton picker. Sometimes we earned money by cotton picking for other folks. One family that we picked cotton for was Mr. Bill Stuart and his son, John Lester.

Usually at the end of a row, we weighed the cotton. A cotton picker was paid by the pound. That was, of course, if you weren't picking for your dad.

After weighing, the cotton was stored in a shed until the farmer felt there was enough to make a bale of between 1100-1300 pounds including the seeds. It was then loaded onto a truck and hauled to a gin. After the seeds were separated from the cotton, at the gin, the cotton was baled and ready for the market. The seeds were also sold to be converted to hulls and meal. In the wintertime farmers would buy back the hulls and meal to feed the cattle.

When we lived at Blackmonton Daddy hauled pulpwood for Mr. Carl Austin. Daddy sometimes had use of Mr. Austin's truck for personal use. This made it possible for Daddy to take us for a ride.

We had a flock of geese. I remember a funny incident about them. We would chase each goose until we caught it, then we sat on a chair with the goose turned upside down between our legs and picked the down feathers. The geese did not like to be picked. They squawked, and bit, too, if they weren't held in a way to prevent this.

One time, Mother decided to run an advertisement in the little paper called the "Market Bulletin," a paper for farm families who wanted to buy or sell something. Offering goose down and feathers for sale, this advertisement brought dozens of post cards from folks wanting to buy the feathers. We had never gotten so much mail, and Mother could not answer all of the cards. Unfortunately she could not supply the orders. She had only enough feathers for two or three customers.

We knew we were poor, but we never were obsessed with it. We had food, clothing, and shelter, though we never owned a home. We attended school every school day, and all of us became members of the middle class society. It did not come easy, but hard work did pay off.

Country living did have its advantages too. We learned to play independently. Friends lived at least a mile away. They had no car, and neither did we. Nor did any of us have a television or telephone.

We never thought of it in such a way, but we were communing with nature. We loved finding the lightning bugs that glowed in the dark, listening to the crickets and the bullfrogs, looking into the heavens for the stars, and the different phases of the moon.

My sister and I played paper dolls by the hour. We cut our paper dolls out of a catalog. Grown-ups and children, and furniture for each room, and then we set them up on our beds.

I was very orderly with this. I would cut furniture for various rooms out of the catalog. When we finished playing, I would place each room in a section of a book so I could then take them out in order the next time. My sister was not nearly so orderly, but when we grew up and had families, she became the orderly one who is the perfect housekeeper, while I became the messy one. Now I love my clutter.

We played make-believe and we made playhouses in just about any hide-away place we could find. We had playhouses in a fallen down old barn, in sheds, under shade trees, and as mentioned we sometimes made a playhouse in our outdoor toilet. Since we were girls, we had to have husbands. We used old broomsticks for husbands, pretending they were various grown men we knew.

Other games that we played were hopscotch, jacks, Rook and Old Maid cards, Monopoly, dominoes, and jump rope. Sometimes we were able to go to Vaiden to a traveling carnival. At the carnival we ate cotton candy, rode the Ferris wheel and the merry-go-round, and had our fortunes told.

Sarah and I liked to play more than we liked to help with the chores. We took advantage of Mother more than Daddy, actually hiding sometimes in the outdoor toilet. One chore that we tried to avoid was washing the dishes. We bargained with mother. "Mother, if you will stack the dishes and wash the pots and pans we will do the rest." This seems ridiculous today, but I remember it well.

At Blackmonton for the first time that I remember, our closest neighbors were not black people. These neighbors lived a greater distance from us than any neighbors had prior to this time.

Blackmonton neighbors included the Roger Shelton Family and the three Stuart Brothers. The Stuarts were Mr. Bill Stuart, his wife Miss Lula, and their son, John Lester; Mr. Ed Stuart his wife Miss Susie, and their adult children J. E. and Susie Opal; and Mr. Claude Stuart and his wife Miss Lottie; Claude and Annie Lois Stuart Bailey.

Our black friends were nearby. They included Parthenia and Cotrell Lofton, their children, and Parthenia's mother. When we moved into the town of Vaiden, Parthenia and Cotrell moved from the country to what was known as the Vaiden place, originally owned by Dr. Vaiden, the namesake of the town of Vaiden.

Parthenia's mother, Alice Moore, was a family friend for life. After I came to New Orleans in 1956, I would return to Vaiden, and if I saw Alice, she was always glad to see me. In those days we called all of the black folks by their first names.

It was while we lived at Blackmonton that my baby brother,-Marvin Cade, was born. Mother went into labor during the night of May 12, 1953, and John Lester Stuart drove her to my grandparents' home in Vaiden. Daddy accompanied them. Sarah Lou, Billy, Bobby, and I stayed home alone. Dr. Herbert Powers home-delivered Marvin Cade on May 13. He weighed 8 pounds 4 ounces. Dwight David Eisenhower, the World War II Commander of the Normandy Invasion and the European theater was in his first term as the 34th president of the United States.

We older children were given the opportunity to name our new baby brother. I was fourteen and took a lead part in his naming. I don't know where the Marvin came from, but one contribution that I made was the Cade. I had remembered that Daddy's oldest brother was named Cade, and for some reason I wanted my brother to have his uncle's name.

Marvin has had various nicknames during his lifetime, but the one that has stuck is "Noggin." This name came about one day when he was two and he hit his head on the black wood burning heater in our grandparents' room. I said to him, you bumped your noggin, hence the name. It seems funny for a grown man to be called "Noggin", but it is probably unique to him and he evidently is proud of the name. He's had many opportunities to change if he didn't like his nickname, but on his desk at a Ford Dealership it says Noggin. I now call him Marvin, as does his wife and mother-in-law, but to many others he is Noggin.

Marvin Cade Noah

Marvin Cade Noah on his Wedding Day
with our Mother December 19, 1976

Although Mother had five children, not one was born at the same place, and each time after I was born, Mother had to make arrangements for the other children. As I record this, I cannot help but wonder how all of the arrangements were made with family, neighbors, and friends when Mother was going to give birth. It causes me to reflect and gives me great appreciation of how hard life must have been for her, but also to note that she had the support of her family, Daddy's family, and friends.

Another big event soon after Marvin's birth was when Mother's parents, Floyd and Maggie Mann, and her Aunt Thelia, moved in with us. We were now a family of ten. I think they were just dropped off with their belongings, as I don't remember them discussing it.

## A Move into the Town of Vaiden

In the fall of 1954 when I was fifteen and a junior in high school, our family moved into the town of Vaiden. This time we landed in a house on the property of my great uncle Mood Randall again.

Vaiden, that small Mississippi town, was a place where, not only God, but also all of the folks around us knew what we were doing. At least, that is the way it seemed. I surely thought the Presbyterian minister, the Reverend Tom Q. Johnston, had some kind of link to God that I didn't have. Much later I learned that Mr. Johnston and I had equal rights with God.

The house that we moved into was the shabbiest house—really a shanty—which we had ever lived in. It was an unpainted frame house with a rusty tin roof. All across the front was a ramshackle porch. This porch did not have the community water bucket, and it was not a gathering place like the other porches had been.

This house was smaller than the one we moved from at Blackmonton. It had three bedrooms, a kitchen, and a fair sized hall where we placed our dining room table. My parents and the three boys were in one bedroom; my sister, Sarah and I slept in another; and my grandparents and great aunt were in the third bedroom. This is where I lived until I came to New Orleans to attend nursing school at Touro Infirmary in 1956.

**Vaiden Front Street Highway 51 1963**

It did have electricity and one faucet for town water. We still had an outdoor toilet where my poor grandfather Floyd spent a lot of time. There was no hot water heater, and we had a wood burning stove, a fireplace in one bedroom, and a large iron heater in the other bedroom.

There were a few advantages, however, to this move. We could walk to church, to school, and to shop for groceries and clothing. There were three dry good stores, a hardware store, a shoe shop, dry cleaners, a post office, several gas stations, a small medical clinic, a bus station, a train depot for freight, our school, a movie theatre, three Protestant churches, all within walking distance.

In the three dry good stores we bought our clothes, shoes and socks, underwear, and any other wearing apparel that we needed. We bought material to make our dresses. There were ready-made dresses too, but I never remember buying one.

There were multiple grocery stores, namely the stores of Mr. Jimmy Fullilove, Mr. Percy Bennett, Mr. Willie Crook, Mr. James Cearley and others. My great-aunt Ruth Pollard also owned a grocery store. Sometimes I would shop for my grandmother's Country Gentleman tobacco at Aunt Ruth's Store, but if the tobacco was a cent cheaper at another store my grandmother, a penny pincher, sent me there. It was from this grandmother that I learned money management.

On some occasions we walked up town on a Saturday afternoon and went to the theatre where movies were shown. We called it "going to the picture show." The movies were cowboy and Indian movies generally. We saw Roy Rogers and Dale Evans and Gene Autry. It was in this movie theatre that I first saw "Song of the South."

Outside the theatre there was a popcorn stand that Mrs. Evelyn Ross, my uncle Sonny Jones' sister, ran. It was a gathering place for some people on Saturday afternoons. Everyone who walked by knew each other, and one by one they would all stop and chat.

Later that same year, "Big Bud," this is what we called Daddy's Uncle Mood, and his wife Aunt Lou moved to Vaiden from New Orleans, becoming our closest neighbors in Vaiden. Lloyd and Christine Welch were our other close neighbors. My grandparents, Tom and Willie Noah, also lived within walking distance.

We lived on the east side of the town across the Illinois Central Railroad Tracks. Both the Shongalo Presbyterian and the Vaiden Methodist Churches were on that side of town. The Presbyterian manse and the

Methodist parsonage were next door to each other. Of those who lived on the east side of town, Presbyterians were in the majority.

We children called the male in the family however he was known, but always with a Mr. before his name. We always called the wife Miss with her name. We rarely called adults by their last names. So it was Miss Margaret and Mr. Vernon (Anderson), Miss Lorraine and Mr. Cade (Armstrong), Miss Eunice and Mr. John (Vandiver), Miss Louise and Mr. Bernard (Sanders), Miss Helen and Mr. Wade (Melton), Mr. Herman and Miss Vera (Johnson), and Miss Lynn Gordon. Some exceptions to the first name rule were Mr. and Mrs. Henry Canon, Dr. and Mrs. Power, and Mrs. Hering, but we called her husband Mr. Joe.

My recall is that one black lady, Mary Winn, and her husband, Roosevelt, lived nearby on the Vandivers' property.

After we moved to Vaiden, my friends and classmates were beginning to drive and I wanted to do the same. Joe Tubeville was teaching one of my friends to drive and agreed to teach me. He had a pick-up truck with a stick shift. I couldn't work the clutch, and didn't learn to drive until I was out of nursing school and took driver's education in Houston, Texas. It was not until I was married that I learned to drive a car with a shift. Nowadays, driving a vehicle with a shift is not a problem.

After moving into the town Vaiden, Daddy planted cotton the next spring. Sarah, Billy, and I, my dad's free labor field hands, helped in our cotton fields, chopping and picking. We also picked cotton for Erskine Vinson. His daughter was in my class at school, but she never did field work.

Although the work was serious and the labor was hard, we talked, sang, and did lots of laughing while picking cotton. However, we were dead tired at the end of a day.

That little town of Vaiden was a safe place to live, and we never worried about locks on our doors or locking up our possessions.

My parents and the rest of the family lived at this place a few more years. From there they moved to the County House when Daddy worked on the Carroll County Roads and to various other places in the Vaiden area. They bought the first and only house they ever owned in the 1970s. That house was sold in 1994, the year Mother broke her leg and later died.

# C. Religious Life

I do not have any kind of emotional or sensational story to tell about my religious life and faith. I am glad, however, that religion has played a part in my life. I am glad that I was exposed to many folks in the church to cheer me on, and that I was not isolated from people of faith.

It was my mother, a Methodist and later a Presbyterian convert, who provided the family with a good serving of religion and made church life important to me.

Growing up in the country and attending activities associated with both the Presbyterian and Methodist Churches, I did not differentiate between the two. I did notice that the Methodists sang louder than the Presbyterians. But that was mainly because my grandfather, Floyd, and his two brothers, Dell and Turner, always sang in the choir at the Enon Methodist Church that we attended. Two other small observations were that the Presbyterians called their minister Mister and we called the Methodist minister Brother and that the Presbyterian minister lived in the manse and the Methodist minister lived in the parsonage.

It was only later in life that I began to understand that the difference was in polity and not in theology. Methodists and Presbyterians believe in the same God.

My sister and I were baptized at the Enon Methodist Church on August 28, 1942. I know that baptism was important to Mother and that she made a special effort to see that all five of her children were baptized.

We were all baptized at the Enon Methodist Church because Mother and her parents were members, and the Presbyterian minister wanted Daddy to be there for the baptism. But Daddy was not a church participant, although. he had joined the Old Salem Presbyterian Church in his youth and his family were active Presbyterians.

At Blackmonton we had church service only once a month as we shared the minister with the Shongalo Presbyterian Church in Vaiden. We did have Sunday school classes every Sunday after Mr. Tom Q. Johnston became the minister. We didn't have a separate building for Sunday school, so all classes were held in various sections of the church. Mrs. Irene Jones, my Uncle Sonny Jones's mother, was my first Sunday school teacher. Hazel Shelton Stuart, a family friend, was kind enough to pick us up and drive us to Sunday school.

In the summer time there were revivals—yes, they had revivals at both the Presbyterian and Methodist Churches. We never called them revivals; we called them "meetings," and we said the meeting is going on at Enon, at New Salem, or at Blackmonton, a Methodist, a Baptist, and a Presbyterian church, respectively. These were all churches out in the country from Vaiden and Carrollton. There were also revivals in the churches in the towns. Everyone who attended these revivals would have agreed that they were spirit-raising events.

It was summertime and it was hot. The country churches had no electricity. There were hand-held fans on all of the church benches. However, no matter the heat, the men wore suits and ties and the women wore hose.

Nor did the hot church deter attendance. Folks took off the week from farm work. The churches were full of people of all denominations since all attended each other's churches.

During the revivals we attended church services morning and night for six straight days and nights. At the end of each church service, we sang what we called an invitational hymn—"Blest Be the Tie That Binds" and "Just as I Am" were two of the hymns that I recall. The songs were sung in an emotional way, and they were an invitation for people to join the church. People got up and walked down the aisle to the front of the church, and we knew they were demonstrating their desire to become a member of that church.

In the summer we also attended Vacation Bible School at the Blackmonton Presbyterian country church and the Shongalo Presbyterian Church in Vaiden. Vacation Bible School was a week-long event. We attended from nine in the morning until noon Monday through Friday.

For one week we studied the Bible, memorized Bible verses, sang, prayed, and played some games. On at least one occasion, Mr. Johnston, the minister, was my class's teacher.

After a week of hard work Bible studying, singing, and some game playing, we had a closing event on Friday night in which the entire community was often invited. We had hayrides, watermelon eating, homemade ice cream or an outdoor picnic.

At some point in my religious upbringing, I memorized the Books of the Bible, the beatitudes that are part of Jesus' teaching to the Galileans found in the Bible, Matthew 5. Here are some of them: Blessed are the merciful, for they shall obtain mercy, blessed are the pure in heart, for they shall see God, blessed are those who hunger and thirst for righteousness, for they shall be satisfied.

I also memorized the Lord's Prayer, and the Apostles' Creed, and many Bible verses and sometimes entire chapters. A couple come to mind: John 3:16 For God so loved the world that he gave his only son, that whosoever believed in him shall have everlasting life, and Psalm 23-The Lord is my shepherd, I shall not want: he makes me lie down in green pastures, he leads me beside still waters, he restores my soul. He leads me in paths of righteousness for his name's sake. Even though I walk through the valley of the shadow of death, I fear no evil: for thou are with me; thy rod and thy staff, they comfort me. Thou preparest a table before me in the presence of my enemies; thou anonintest my head with oil, my cup overflows. Surely goodness and mercy shall follow me all the days of my life; and I shall dwell in the house of the Lord forever.

One big summer church event was the Enon Methodist Church Homecoming-called Dinner on the Grounds in those days. This event took place on a Saturday in May so that the men could clean the graves while women set up pot luck food under the trees. This was an occasion that we generally knew we would go shopping for a new dress and a new pair of shoes.

Mr. Johnston was the minister at the Blackmonton Presbyterian Church when I graduated from the eighth grade. He put lots of pressure on me to join the church. It wasn't that I did not have an interest in doing do, but I was just too timid-actually afraid—of getting up in front of people in the church. However, my sister and I joined the Blackmonton Presbyterian Church that summer.

I remember it well; Mr. Johnston had approached Mother and me over and over about church membership. Daddy was never approached. Daddy never went to church except to occasional funerals. I only remember seeing Daddy at his mother's, his daddy's, and my mother's funeral. He surely was at other funerals, but I have no memory of it.

Though I did record in my diary on August 4, 1957, during a vacation home from nursing school that Daddy went to church. To have recorded it must have meant that it was an unusual happening.

On March 20, 1955, my sister and I transferred our membership from the Blackmonton Presbyterian Church to Shongalo Presbyterian Church in Vaiden, and there it remained until I moved my membership in 1972 to the Lakeview Presbyterian Church in New Orleans, Louisiana.

We had a very active and well attended Sunday school class at the Shongalo Presbyterian Church. Mrs. Margaret Anderson—we called her Miss Margaret" was our teacher and her relief was Mrs. Gladys Hatcher—we called her Miss Gladys. I don't remember Miss Margaret ever missing a class. She used this well-worn Bible that she had used for years for reference, but we had regular Sunday school books to study.

In her class I remember we focused on the teachings of the New Testament. In earlier Sunday school classes, we studied Catechism for Young Children. I still have my copy. Some of the questions and answers: 1.) Who made you? God 2.) What else did God make? God made all things. There were a total of 145 questions.

# D. School Life

## Blackmonton School

Either in late August or early September 1944, I started to school at the Blackmonton Country School. My parents didn't have to consider which school that I would attend. Blackmonton was the only school.

The school was segregated then, and I never attended an integrated school until I went back to college in the 1970s at the University of New Orleans. Blackmonton was a country school that had three classrooms. It dwindled down to two rooms prior to my transfer to Vaiden School. It eventually became a one teacher school, and in the early 1950s it was closed.

Our water came from a well that had a pump, and in my first few years we always had to take our lunch. Later we did have a lunchroom and my grandmother, Willie, was one of the lunchroom workers.

That same September that I started school, another big event happened in my life. My brother, Billy Layne, was born on September 18, 1944.

My first school bus driver was Mr. Joe Shelton. His school bus was a pick up truck that had a covered bed on the back with benches on each side. Because of the birth of my new baby brother, I sat in front in the cab with Mr. Joe. Mr. Joe went to Greenwood every Saturday, and sometimes we would get a ride to Greenwood with him.

My first teacher was Miss Lillie Hatcher. She was a Mississippi native who grew up in the Blackmonton Community, and she was formerly a student at that same school.

Her students called her Miss Lillie. Miss Lillie was a kind and gentle teacher. She may have used a paddle, but I don't remember. However, she used "standing in the corner" as a method of disciplining her students.

My own personal experience follows. It says something about my behavior. I was likely a "Jack in the Box" just as I am today. One winter day, I got up from my seat, asked Miss Lillie if I could go to the outdoor toilet. She did not grant me permission and made me stand on one foot. I wet my pants, and Miss Lillie had to dry them by the wood heater.

I always hung on to the name Miss Lillie. She was a loveable teacher. I stayed in touch with her until I left for nursing school and even afterward when I saw her in Vaiden. I remember her with fondness.

The education that I received at Blackmonton was not sophisticated. We concentrated almost exclusively on reading, writing (printing at first) and arithmetic. During reading class, those of us in the same grade sat in our little chairs in a semi-circle around Miss Lillie. My first reading book was called "Winky." I remember reading "Winky run and Winky run, run, run. See Winky run". Another early reader was "Faces and Places." In this book we learned the song "Home on the Range."

It was, also, in the small collection of books that we had at Blackmonton that I was first introduced to Mark Twain's *Tom Sawyer* and *Huckleberry Finn.*

We didn't have art, music, or any organized sports. Much of the learning was rote. I memorized the presidents of the United States, the state capitals, and the Gettysburg Address, all of which I still can recite more that fifty years after memorizing them at that small rural country school. As an elementary student my daughter Gionne was accustomed to impressing her friends with my ability to rattle off the presidents of the United States.

At Blackmonton we played in the yard until the bell rang. After hearing the bell, we lined up in the front yard by the steps. We walked orderly into the classroom.

In the fourth and fifth grades, my last two years at Blackmonton, I had a different teacher, Louise Jones Walker, a sister-in-law of my Aunt Ruby Noah Jones.

At some point in our Blackmonton School days my sister and I got head lice. I remember how horrified my Aunt Ruth was that we had lice. We were told that we likely got it from a fellow student—name withheld—while we were squatting in the school line with this unnamed person's coat over our heads to keep warm.

School was not all work. We had a small stage, and the first play I ever saw was at Blackmonton School. Grace Elliott was the lead character—Goldilocks—in *The Three Bears*. Though memory dims, that little play remains in my mind and what a wonderful little fairy tale.

Though we had no electricity, we had night events. One was a Halloween celebration. We pinned the tale on the donkey blindfolded, and we bobbed for apples in a tub of water. No one worried about how sanitary bobbing for apples may be.

We learned the traditional Christmas carols, like It Came upon the Midnight Clear, Joy to the World, and Silent Night.

During recess and at lunchtime, we played games that required our imagination only, hopscotch with shards of glass to throw into the blocks, jump rope alone and with a person on each end to throw the rope while others jumped until they missed.

We sometimes threw the rope fast, and we called this hot pepper and at other times we would throw the rope at a regular pace. One of the little sayings that the rope throwers would say to the person jumping the rope was Cinderella dressed in yellow went to town to meet her fellow, and as she jumped the persons throwing the rope would count how many kisses she would get. Other games were Ring Around the Rosey, London Bridge, Mother May I, Drop the Handkerchief, and Hide and Seek.

Classmates who I remember at Blackmonton are Paul Shelton, Gloria Faye Minyard, Denon McNeil McGraw, Shirley Marie Goss, and Robbie Brooks. Paul Shelton is the only classmate who started to school with me at Blackmonton, went through the fifth grade there and both of us transferred to the Vaiden in the sixth grade. We were in school the entire twelve years together.

## Vaiden School

I do not know why, but in the fall of 1949 Sarah Lou and I transferred from Blackmonton Country School to the Vaiden School. I was in the sixth grade, and she was in the third. Some of the other students remained in the Blackmonton School and others transferred to the Vaiden School as we did.

My parents made the decision, but they were never involved in my school in any way other than Mother signing my report card. Making that transfer was a big adjustment for me. The new environment sometimes felt hostile, and I was afraid of failure.

Mr. Roger Shelton was our school bus driver. We traveled on dirt roads and gravel roads in a big yellow school bus furnished by the Carroll County School System. We never got stuck in the mud, the school bus never broke down, and we didn't ever have a flat tire.

Mr. Roger's son Paul was in my class. Paul had rheumatic fever when we were in the fourth or fifth grade at Blackmonton. He stayed out of school for months because of his illness, but was never held back a grade.

Miss Gladys was Mr. Roger's wife. She was a lunchroom worker who rode the school bus with us. Miss Gladys sat in the first seat on the driver's side by Mr.Roger, smoking and chatting with Mr. Roger. My memories of this school bus ride are clear. We behaved, and I don't ever remember a fight. If there was any kind of disturbance, Mr. Roger would look up into the mirror, call a person's name and all would become quiet.

We arose at dawn and were ready and standing on the road to wait on the school bus by 7 a.m. We stood on the road and waited for the school bus, rain or shine. Mr. Roger expected us to be there when he arrived, and we were, I think, 100 per cent of the time. I clearly remember that he had to wait on some of the students, but their house was close enough to the road so that Mr. Roger could see them coming, and they took their good old time. We arrived at school by 8 a.m.for the school bell.

On the school bus we often sang songs and sometimes talked international politics. One song that I remember was "Some Glad Morning." Part of the first verse went like this. "Some glad morning when this life is over, I'll fly away, I'll fly away, oh glory I'll fly away."

When Joseph Stalin died, we discussed his death on the school bus. We realized he was some kind of bad man if not the "Bad Man" we learned about in Sunday school.

At Blackmonton we had oil lamps and outdoor toilets. At Vaiden we had electricity and indoor toilets.

**Carolyn Sue Noah**
**Grade 5 Blackmonton School**

**Sarah Lou Noah**
**Grade 3 Vaiden School**

Whereas I was accustomed to one teacher for three grades, I now had three teachers for one grade. One teacher for math, one for social studies, and another teacher for other subjects was tension-producing for me. Mrs. Kittrell taught geography and health, Mrs. Muse taught math, and Miss Grace taught spelling and English. I don't remember one thing that I learned.

This change of schools was traumatic in so many ways. My teachers did not help with the trauma I was experiencing. I know Blackmonton teachers were family friends and about the same age of my parents. Except for Miss Grace, my parents had never even heard of my sixth grade teachers.

Mrs. Kittrell was the meanest teacher I had ever known and the meanest one I ever had after that time. Though I must admit anybody would have scared me if they looked at me straight. In health class, one of the assignments was to check fingernails, shoe polishing, and other grooming activities. There was a little chart that hung on the wall, and there were various colored stars that you received depending upon your grooming. Gold stars meant you were as good as you could get, or that your grooming was perfect. I worked hard at having all in order. On one of the checks I had gotten the gold star, but was too short to reach the place on the chart where it belonged. A classmate offered to place it for me, but of placing it on my spot, she placed it on hers. Mrs. Kittrell was not sympathetic when I tried to remedy the problem. She chose to do nothing about it. But I know I was devastated that I missed getting that gold star. Mrs. Kittrell was still in the Vaiden School System after I came to New Orleans, and when I went back to the school for some reason, she was quite nice to me. But I will always remember her as the meanest teacher that I ever came into contact with as a young person or at any time.

Miss Grace was a local person, an old maid, who continued to live with her parents, and the first person I ever knew who wore a hearing aid. She was the first teacher I knew who had teacher's pets," who she treated in a special way, and she often scared me, probably because I was so afraid of a teacher saying boo to me. She, too, was much nicer to me when I came home from New Orleans to visit. We even attended the same church and she came to a birthday party that Mother gave for me on one of my trips back home.

Mrs. Muse was the nicest of my teachers the year I made the transfer from Blackmonton to Vaiden, the only teacher who didn't crush my weakened ego state. But I didn't let those teachers, Mrs. Kittrell and Miss Grace," ruin my zest for learning.

I never got a spanking at school, but one time Mrs. Ely, a seventh grade teacher, paddled my hand with a ruler when I lost my place in what was being read in English class. That is the only disciplinary measure that I can recall from that time forth.

After transferring to the Vaiden School, Billy, Sarah Lou and I had to walk to our Noah grandparent's home to eat lunch. It was only about a mile to my grandparent's house, but seemed further.

My grandmother cooked for my grandfather, who ate at a different time, and she cooked for the three of us for over five years. Rain or shine, hot or cold, if we had lunch, we had to walk to get it. The lunch was always on the table when we arrived and we didn't help with cleaning the kitchen after we ate. We had to hurry back to school. I don't recall ever skipping lunch. When my parents moved into the town of Vaiden, we lived close enough to school to walk home for lunch.

Lunchtime was a time for play and interaction for our peers, but I would get back from lunch late. When we got back from lunch, it was sometimes hard to go up to a little group of people, and try to socialize with them.

By eighth grade, two years later, I felt somewhat assimilated into the Vaiden School. In the spring of 1952, my class had an eighth grade graduation. We wore a cap and gown similar to the ones that we would wear as a high school senior.

As an eighth grade graduation surprise present, I was able to take a trip to Gulfport, Mississippi. My Aunt Verna, "Sister," her husband, and daughter, Janice came to visit us, and I went home with them for a week. I rode a Trailways bus back home. That was the first time I had ridden in any transportation other than a school bus or someone's private vehicle. Nineteen fifty-two was a big year.

## High School

It was really in the ninth grade that I began class participation with confidence. I realized that if I read the subject and participated in class, it meant a difference in my grade. You could call me a late bloomer or precocious, depending how you look at it. Some children, including mine, did not begin to study until college, but I began to realize studying and making good grades was important to me early in my high school years.

We needed sixteen credit hours to graduate from Vaiden High School. That meant we had four subjects each of the four years of high school, with English required each of the four years. Miss Shula Armstrong was my English teacher all four years.

We had grammar and conjugation drilled into us so much and so often that even a mentally challenged, uninterested student could get it. In my brain those conjugation lessons are easily retrieved. An example of the verb infinitive—to see—present tense singular I see (never ever I seen), you see, he, she, it sees, plural we see, you see, they see, past tense I saw, you saw, he, she, it saw, we saw, you saw, they saw: future tense: I will see, you will see, he, she, it will see, we will see, you will see, they will see.

There were many more verb tenses and many more rules. Knowing these tenses made learning a foreign language as a college student without any prior foreign language experience much easier. For that I can thank Miss Shula.

Miss Shula was also noted for Monday morning sharing of current events and for lengthy lectures on proper behavior. One afternoon Miss Shula, who was never married, talked to us about smooching and said no one better be caught smooching. As far as she was concerned, it was not allowed even in private.

We also heard the horror news stories from Miss Shula. Mrs. Moselle Nelms was killed by a Freedom Rider. Mrs. Nelms' husband had refused to serve the Freedom Rider and had threatened him. We didn't understand it all, but we were saddened about Mrs. Nelms leaving two little boys without a mother.

Another sad story also had to do with a murder. "Nookie" Bennett, in Memphis, Tennessee, had been killed by her boy friend, John Hill. Both were from Vaiden, and Nookie's parents, Mr. Percy and Miss Maggie Bennett, owned a grocery store in Vaiden.

It is interesting to note that Miss Shula married Mr. Percy after his wife died. This is not to imply that they, in fact, had been involved in any kind of immoral behavior prior to the death of Mr. Percy's wife. Miss Shula is a memorable person in my life and the influence she had upon my learning proper grammar is immeasurable.

Another memorable subject was home economics, but it is more memorable for what I didn't learn than what I did. However, this was not the teacher's fault. Miss Carithers was our teacher. She was kind, she was enthusiastic about her calling to be a teacher, and she was helpful. But I must take the responsibility for my own lack of talent and enthusiasm.

I thought I was to prepare to be domestic. That was a mistake, as I never learned to sew, never liked to sew, and hope nothing in my future depends upon my sewing ability. Reluctantly, I will thread a needle to sew on a missing button. The cooking I learned was not anything practical and nothing I needed a class for anyway. I did learn to set the table properly and how to fold a napkin.

What I did learn was that "Home Ec" as we called it needed a different kind of inspiration than I had and that, indeed, generations before me had learned not from classes, but from their mothers, and my mother did not inspire me to cook and sew.

I did learn house cleaning, washing and ironing, and other domestic activities from Mother. I often took those responsibilities readily but I didn't need a class to learn them. However, one of the enjoyments was being in the good graces of the home economics teacher, Miss Carithers, so that in the afternoons during study hall some of us girls received permission to go to the home economics building to do cleaning. That was a good excuse for getting out of study hall.

In the ninth grade I took civics, math, home economics, and English, in the tenth grade I took English, home economics, Algebra I, and a geography course that I have not one thing that I can recollect. It must have been taught by a football coach and all I have in my recollection about those courses taught by football coaches is that our class, at least, two days in a week, consisted of football and football again and again or whatever sport was in season.

In my junior year, I took English, American history—didn't learn any history at that time but later in life history has been an important hobby—typing-which I never thought was of any benefit until computers came into my life and again home economics which was allowed in the place of geometry. As a senior I took English IV, bookkeeping, Algebra II and chemistry.

Some of the school related activities were recreational. Mr. Roger on occasions drove us to school activities using the Carroll County school bus. We went to basketball and football games. I remember we lived about two miles below Mr. Roger, and he told us if we could get to his house, he'd drive the school bus to the game. That sounds like a nice way to get exercise today, but we didn't like it much at the time nor did we think about walking being a good thing for your health. After all, he was using the school bus provided by the county, and it was of no expense to him. I suppose these are the things people come to resent later in life. But for me, this is not the case, as I am happy to have escaped the dependency. Furthermore, it gives one great pride to know that more independence was accomplished with one's own motivation.

Vaiden always seemed to have a winning girls' basketball team. In those days the girls' teams played differently from the boys. On one end of the court you had the girls who were forwards with the opposing team's guards. Only the forwards made the goals for the teams, and if you were a team member you were either a forward or a guard, never both.

At other times my Aunt Ruby Jones and her husband Sonny took us to football games. We sent them a note asking them to take us to a game, and they usually did. Sometimes we stayed at my grandparents' home in Vaiden and their neighbor, Miss Helen and her husband, Mr. Wade Melton, drove us to the in town school games.

Other school-sponsored activities included cakewalks, and one time the Lions Club on had a womanless wedding. On rare occasions we had a dance. I always felt awkward trying to dance. Mother could dance very well, and she told me I didn't have rhythm. I didn't need her to tell me that, but she did. That made my self-consciousness even worse. But I did like to participate in the Virginia Reel. We didn't need a partner for that so even wallflowers were able to dance the Virginia Reel.

Cakewalks were usually held to raise money. Various folks in the town made cakes for this fundraiser. These walks were held in the gym where a large circle was drawn. Some of the specifics are foggy to me, but here's what I remember. You paid a price to walk, the music would start, and you walked around until the music stopped, and whoever landed on a certain number would get a cake. I guess that happened until all of the cakes were taken.

The entire school went to the auditorium regularly on Fridays for a song fest of patriotic songs, prayer, announcements, and during football season, for pep rallies. Mr. Frank Prewitt was the school superintendent, and he decided what we needed to hear. We went to the auditorium in an orderly procession, and we were on our best behavior while there.

I was never a cheerleader or class officer and I didn't play sports other than volley ball, I was in the Beta Club, 4-H Club, and I was in both the junior and senior class plays.

I am still in possession of both of the scripts. The junior play was "The Valley of Ghosts," and my character was Lily Violet. Lily was a Negress about 25. I had to paint my face black for three nights in a row. She is much blonder than Sally Ann, and goes in for the same elaborate rouging of lips and cheeks. Both are elaborately dressed in cheap, flashy street clothes and high heels. We practiced these plays night after night and they were polished and perfected to the point that we didn't miss a line.

The senior play was entitled "Finders Creepers." I had the part of Nina Quigley, 13. "She, too, is a cute and sweet little girl, and the bright spot in Hercules' usually blackened eye. Also wears a skirt and sweater." At least the class sponsors thought I was cute.

In March of 1956 our senior class and our class sponsor, Mr. Tom Dulin, took a senior trip. Mr. Dulin's wife, "Bootsy" and Mrs. Prewitt went along with Mr. Dulin as chaperones.

Earlier in the school year we sold magazines and had other fundraisers to raise money for the trip, my first trip out of the state of Mississippi. This first stop was Montgomery, Alabama where we saw the First White House of the Confederacy. From there we went to Panama City, Florida, where most of us saw snow white beach sand for the first time, then we went to Silver Springs, Florida, where we took a ride in glass bottom boats and saw huge turtles.

Our final destination was Daytona Beach, Florida. This first traveling experience whetted my desire for seeing places and doing things. I have now traveled from the Atlantic to the Pacific, from the Gulf of Mexico to the Great Lakes, to Mexico, Canada, to Germany and to Rio de Janeiro, Brazil.

On April 19, 1956, my class of thirty-three graduated from Vaiden High School. That fall six of my classmates went to colleges in Mississippi, and I entered nursing school in New Orleans, Louisiana.

# Chronology

| | |
|---|---|
| 1938 | Carolyn Sue Noah, daughter of Robert and "Dollie" Mann Noah was born on December 29, 1938, in the Blackmonton Community of Carroll County, Mississippi. That same year Adolph Hitler appointed himself War Minister of Germany, marched into Austria and claimed Austria as part of Germany. That same year the Munich Pack was signed by Britain, France and Italy. The Munich Pack allowed Germany to partition Czechoslovakia. |
| 1939 | On September 03, 1939, Great Britain and France declared war on Germany beginning World War II. |
| 1939 | On May 10, 1940, Winston Churchill became Prime Minister of Great Britain following the resignation of Neville Chamberlain. |
| 1939 | June 10, 1940, Italy declared war on Great Britain and France. |
| 1941 | May 6, 1941, Joseph Stalin became Soviet Premier. War was literally world wide, but our country was still isolationistic. |
| 1941 | Sarah Lou Noah, daughter of Robert and Dollie Mann Noah, was born on December 1, 1941, in the Enon Community of Carroll County, Mississippi. |
| 1941 | December 7, 1941,—my sister was seven days old—when the naval and air force of Japan attacked the United States naval base at Pearl Harbor. President Roosevelt's quote regarding the attack. "Yesterday December 7, 1941, a date which will live in infamy, the United States of America was suddenly and deliberately attacked by naval and air forces of the Empire of Japan." On December 8, the United States declared war on Japan. On December 11, Germany and Italy, allies of Japan declared war on the United States. |
| 1941 | Research began on making the atomic bomb. It was called the Manhattan Project. After scientists found out that radioactive materials would be used to make a bomb, President Franklin Roosevelt responded by creating the Uranium Committee to investigate this possibility. At Oak Ridge, Tennessee, the desired uranium-235 was separated from the more abundant uranium-238, and at the Hanford, Washington installation |

nuclear reactors were built to transmute nonfissionable uranium into plutonium-239. The actual design and building of the bomb took place at Los Alamos, New Mexico under the leadership of J. Oppenheimer, an American physicist.

1942 Robert and Dollie Noah with their two children, Carolyn Sue and Sarah Lou, moved to the Old Salem Community into a house on Robert's grandfather's property according to Dell Lee, Robert's first cousin. We called it the John Lee Place because the John Lee family formerly lived there.

1944 On June 6, 1944, during in World War II the United States and its British Allies invaded the European continent through Normandy, France in a plan known as Operation Overlord. The plan had been prepared since 1943 and the supreme command over its execution was entrusted to General Dwight David Eisenhower. In May 1944, bombing was begun in order to destroy German communications in Northern France. Just after midnight on June 6, British and American airborne forces landed behind the German coastal fortifications known as the Atlantic Wall. They were followed after daybreak by the seaborne troops of the United States 1st Army and British 2nd Army. Field Marshal B. L. Montgomery was in command of the Allied land forces. Some 4,000 transports, 800 warships, and innumerable small craft, under Admiral Sir B. H. Ramsay, supported the invasion. More than 1100 aircraft, under Air Chief Marshal Sir Trafford Leigh-Mallory, formed a protective umbrella. While naval guns and Allied bombers assaulted the beach fortifications, the men swarmed ashore. The German commander, Field Marshal Gerd von Rundstedt, found that Allied air strength prevented use of his reserves. The U. S. 3rd Army under General George S. Patton broke through the German left flank at Avranches. Finally the German 7th Army was caught in the "Falaise pocket" and this wiped the Germans out by August 23, opening the way for the Allies to overrun Northern France.

1944 On September 18, 1944, Billy Layne Noah—third child and first son of Robert and Dollie Mann Noah—was born near Black Hawk in Carroll County, Mississippi.

1945    On April 12, 1945, President Franklin Delano Roosevelt (FDR) died in Warm Springs, Georgia of a cerebral hemorrhage (stroke)

1945    On April 12, 1945, Harry S Truman, the Vice-President became the President of the United States. He had scarcely seen President Roosevelt and had received no briefing on the development of the atomic bomb nor of the developing difficulties with Soviet Russia. President Truman told reporters. "I felt like the moon, stars, and all of the planets had fallen on me."

1945    On July 6, 1945, President Harry Truman left for Potsdam, Germany, for a meeting with Soviet Premier Stalin and British Prime Ministers Winston Churchill and Atlee. The Potsdam Conference was held from July 16-August 2, 1945. At this conference post-war arrangements in Europe were discussed frequently, without agreement. Future moves against Japan were also discussed. Another result of the conference was a July 26 joint proclamation by the United States, Great Britain, and China regarding Japan. The "Potsdam described Japan's present perilous condition, gave the terms for her surrender, and stated the Allies' intention concerning her postwar status. It ended with an ultimatum: Japan must immediately agree to unconditionally surrender, or face "prompt and utter destruction.

1945    The nuclear test explosion took place in Alamogordo, New Mexico on July 16, 1945.

1945    Allies broadcast demand that Japan surrender or face destruction on July 28th.

1945    First scheduled day for dropping the bomb on Japan was August 3, 1945, weather permitting.

1945    The first uranium bomb "Little Boy," was dropped on Hiroshima on August 6, 1945, killing 70,000 Japanese inhabitants. Three days later on August 9, 1945, a plutonium bomb was dropped on Nagasaki, killing 35,000 or more inhabitants.

1945    Japan surrendered to the United States on August 14, 1945, ending World War II.

1945-1989 Cold War with Russia

1947      Robert Mann "Bobby" Noah, son of Robert and Dollie Mann Noah was born on March 4, 1947, in Vaiden, Mississippi, at the home of Robert's brother and his wife, Ken and Louise. It was a big year for world wide historical events. The Truman Doctrine was introduced. This was a pledge by the United States to combat the spread of Communism and to assist any nation fighting Communist insurgency. This desire over the next two decades led the United States into the Korean and Vietnam Conflicts. That same year the Marshall Plan was introduced. This plan offered aid from the United States to the nations of Europe to assist with recovery from World War II. The countries that participated requested $17 billion in assistance over a four-year period. This plan opened European markets to American trade like never before and the door was opened to American domination of the global economy. This $17 billion is widely regarded as the greatest investment in American history.

1947      It was an eventful year for India in that Mahatma Gandhi's Civil Disobedience led to India's independence from England. Still another important event of 1947 was the publishing of *The Diary of Anne Frank*. Anne Frank, a Jew, was born in Germany and fled with her family to Amsterdam in 1933 to escape Nazi persecution. After the Nazis occupied Holland, her family hid for three years (1942-1944) in a sealed-off room above a warehouse. During those years, Anne kept a diary. The family was betrayed to the Germans in 1944, and Anne died in the Bergen-Belsen concentration camp. In 1947 her father found the diary and had it published. It became a bestseller, was translated into English in 1953 and was eventually translated into thirty languages.

1950-1953 Korean War, June 25, 1950, to July 27, 1953. At the end of World War II, Korea was divided at the 38th parallel into Soviet (North Korean) and U. S. (South Korean) zones of occupation. Relations between the two Koreas became strained, and on June 25, 1950, North Korean forces invaded South Korea. The United Nations quickly condemned the invasion as an act of aggression, demanded the withdrawal of North Korean troops from the South, and called upon its members to aid South Korea.

1952    In 1952 Dwight David Eisenhower was selected as the Republican nominee for the President of the United States. Adlai Stevenson was the Democratic nominee. Eisenhower chose Richard Milhous Nixon, U.S. Senator from California as his vice-president running mate.

1953    Marvin Cade Noah, last child and third son of Robert and "Dollie" Mann Noah, was born on May 13, 1953, in the home of Robert's parents in Vaiden, Mississippi. That same year J. Robert Oppenheimer, a designer of the atomic bomb was suspended by the Atomic Energy Commission as an alleged security risk.

# Chapter 6  My Journey as a Student Nurse

## A Dream

As a small child in the second grade at the Blackmonton Country School in Carroll County, Mississippi, I began to have childhood dreams about becoming a nurse. I can still see myself in that big dream—a nurse spick and span in a starched, stiff, white uniform, white stockings, and white laced oxford shoes, a white nurse's cap, and a smile. That was a captured moment in my memory, there to remain even 50 plus years later, though times have changed.

Whether by fate, will power, voice from an old dream, or the intervention of some higher spiritual power, I took chemistry as a senior in high school. A nurse was born, but I didn't know it. Never did I voice my dream to anyone, but there was that voice inside me, "Take that chemistry."

I responded to that inner voice and took chemistry, known to be the most difficult class in high school. That was the beginning of a journey that I would take in September 1956 when I entered the Touro Infirmary School of Nursing in New Orleans.

There were only eight out of 32 of us Vaiden High School seniors brave enough to take that course. Classmates I remember include Lucretia Applewhite, Larry Randle, and Nicky Oliver. Lucretia and I have remained friends, and in the year 2000 she shared a chemistry experience with me. "I used to vomit every morning just thinking about chemistry class." Mr. Frank Prewitt, the feared and revered high school principal, was the chemistry teacher. Under Mr. Prewitt I learned through fear that if I persevered I could do most anything I set my heart and mind to do.

Chemistry class
dream reality
in a nutshell

I am eternally grateful for that high school chemistry experience. It prepared me well for my college chemistry class. In fact, chemistry was my easiest subject as a first year nursing student, thus making time for other subjects and for becoming adjusted to a very large city for this real small town country girl. This was important. Fellow students in my nursing school class who really wanted to become nurses and would have made wonderful nurses flunked out of nursing school because they failed chemistry, microbiology, or some other academic subject. In a diary entry on May 23, 1957, I wrote, "Six failed microbiology. Billie failed psychology." I didn't record the chemistry failures.

Though I was beginning to prepare myself, I never told anyone about my dream to become a nurse until late summer after high school graduation. That's when I began to discuss wanting to go to nursing school with my mother.

The summer after high school graduation a discussion came after a six week trek to Cicero, Illinois (Al Capone's mobster city, but of this I was unaware), with a high school classmate, Sarah Alice Vinson, and her new husband, "Dub" Huggins. In Cicero I worked as a clerk at the International Harvester Plant, and Northern guys, likely flirting, although I didn't realize it, brought me watermelons to get me to talk Southern. That was easy; that's all I knew.

In Cicero I received my first marriage proposal, not from one of the Northern guys, but from the brother of Sarah Alice's husband. I don't even remember his name. That was so crazy that it seems like it didn't happen. We hadn't even known each other for more than a month. I think he was serious, but I laughed.

After that Northern trek and my discussion with Mother, we began to talk about the need for financial assistance. My first beacon of light was a bank loan from the Holmes County Bank and Trust signed by my father, Robert Noah; paternal grandfather, Tom Noah; my great uncle, Mood Randall; and my grandmother, Willie Mae Randall's, first cousin Plunkett Johnson. This made it possible for me to get on a train in Winona, Mississippi, come to New Orleans, and enroll in nursing school at Touro Infirmary. Why I chose to come to New Orleans and why I chose the Touro Infirmary School of Nursing is not in my memory bank.

When the opportunity struck, I heard the voice of my old dream, I responded, and this changed my life's path. That first hurdle had been negotiated. Every thing now depended upon my own gumption and personal initiative.

After graduation from nursing school I faithfully repaid the bank loan of less than $1000 for the entire three years at $50 a month until the loan was fully paid. The risk the bank took and the risk of those who signed the bank note made possible a path in life for me that no one could have imagined from a child born of uneducated, poor but hardworking parents.

By the time I was ready to leave for New Orleans on my first trip to this city on the Mississippi River that late summer of 1956, a larger community knew of my desire. Everyone must have expected me to be accepted into nursing school. My grandmother, Willie Randall Noah, her cousin, Bessie Johnson Rogers, and my grandmother's neighbor, Lynn Tucker Gordon, began sewing for me in preparation for the trip to New Orleans. From that time forth there was no turning back. I cannot begin to fathom what my life would have been like had I not come to New Orleans to nursing school.

I left Vaiden, my family, my church, my friends, everything that I loved, not because I was in a hurry to get away, but because opportunity knocked at my door, and I wanted to enter to fulfill a dream of my early childhood. No one could go through that door for me. I, myself, had to enter.

My great Aunt Lou, Big Bud's wife, a native of New Orleans but our neighbor in Vaiden when I left for New Orleans, Mother, and my little three year old brother, Noggin, and Aunt Lou told me goodbye and perhaps other members of my family told me goodbye too, but they were not in the photograph with that final goodbye.

With my first bank account in my name and some blank checks I was ready to leave that small town life. Daddy drove me to the train station in Winona in Big Bud's fancy Chrysler car. Daddy took me reluctantly because he wanted me to get a job and help support the family. In Winona I got on a train headed for New Orleans, my suitcases packed with most everything that I owned. Daddy had let go of his parental responsibilities at that moment and never once did he try to discourage me again. I was emancipated without any strings attached.

In New Orleans, my Aunt Lou's niece, Mina LaGrange Windecker, met me at the train station in New Orleans. Prior to that time I had met Mina in Vaiden on one occasion. Mina soon became a friend. She took me to the apartment where she lived with her parents, Pete and Corrine LaGrange, on South Prieur Street in New Orleans to spend the night.

Also, I knew Louise "Bookie" Shelton and Betty Cummins, who, by the time I arrived, was married to Ronnie Clark. Both were girls from my hometown who were Touro Infirmary School of Nursing graduates. Though I knew them I had not seen either of them in years, and they had nothing to do with my nursing school choice.

I have no recall of why I wanted to enroll in the Touro Infirmary School of Nursing or why I decided to travel to New Orleans. I do remember Big Bud, who had lived in New Orleans for years, had suggested Charity Hospital of Nursing. But I never once considered Charity. On August 27, 1956, I wrote my first note in my diary that I kept almost daily from then through October 25, 1958. "I came to Touro Infirmary to start a pre-entrance program. I am scared to death. I pray I will pass the test." On August 28, "Took the pre-entrance test today. Praying I passed and will be excepted (yes I wrote excepted, not accepted) at Touro. A little homesick."

On August 29 I wrote, "Well, this was one of those days. I passed the pre-entrance exam in the school of nursing. Thankful." God was smiling down on me and in this case my prayer was answered as I had asked. It was an adrenalin filled moment. I was aware that my opportunity had arrived, and that I must reach out and seize it.

My world changed. I knew I must open my mind to receive the world beyond my childhood. Though scared, frightened, overwhelmed, and excited, I was relieved, and I was thrilled. I was even sad that it would be a long while before I would see my family. All of this was intermingling within me.

## Brief History of Touro

Judah Touro, a Sephardic Jew, arrived in New Orleans from Rhode Island in 1802, about a year prior to the Louisiana Purchase in 1803, at the age of 27. He invested in ice houses, oceangoing ships, and real estate and became quite wealthy. He died in 1854, but prior to his death he made a will for a clinic and infirmary to serve the unfortunate.

The clinic's original location at South Peters and Clio Streets was in the heart of the city's shipping activities and accessible to the major steamboat landings of the time. The hospital closed during the Civil War and reopened on January 3, 1869. In 1882 the hospital moved to its present location on Prytania Street between Foucher and Aline Streets. This new facility designated accommodations for private patients, but has continued to serve clinic patients.

According to the Touro Infirmary annual report of 1869-1870, the first Touro nurses were men. It was not until October 1, 1896, that the Touro Infirmary Training School for Nurses became a reality. Miss Frances Quaife, formerly of Bellevue Hospital, New York, was employed as the Superintendent of the Hospital and Director of Nurses.

Due to the need for someone to take care of the steady increase of female patients, five women had been employed to practice nursing prior to the opening of the nursing school. When the school was opened, these women became the senior nursing students. Terms of admission to the school were "Candidates should be women between the ages of 24 and 36 years of age, possessing a good common school education and must furnish certificates of good character, good health, with mental and physical capacity for the duties of nursing.

## Who Were We and the Student Nurse Experience

I didn't sever my ties or my identity with my hometown or my family. But with one identity I was called by four different names during my nursing school days. I was Sue to my hometown folks; I was Noah to my fellow classmates; I was called Miss Noah—we were all required to introduce ourselves to the patients, doctors, and other staff by our last names with the miss attached—by the patients and instructors; and Carolyn by other folks that I met along the way. I also answered to Carol or Caroline.

My classmates and I were 56 young, unmarried women between the ages of 17 and 19 just out of high school except for one or two of us. Most of us entered the nursing profession for altruistic reasons. We were dedicated women who were there for the noble cause of serving the sick, ministering to those experiencing grief, and my personal conviction was then and is now that I could make a difference. For me it was a sacred calling. I had the zeal of a foreign missionary.

On August 30 and 31, I wrote about touring the hospital and going to a lecture on the "Do's and Do not's." That weekend I went to Mina's.

On Saturday, September 2, I wrote "Mina, Bernice and family and I took a ride across Lake Pontchartrain, longest bridge in the world today." That bridge, called the Causeway, is 24 miles long and the world's longest bridge of its kind. On Sunday, September 3, 1956, I attended church at the Canal Street Presbyterian Church.

That night I went to the Touro Infirmary School of Nursing Residence located at 3450 Chestnut Street in New Orleans, my home for the next three years. It was called the Selma Gumbel Nurses Residence, a building that was dedicated on October 19, 1955. It was a facility that was built to house all of the Touro Infirmary student nurses on the third through eighth floors and to accommodate capping and graduation exercises. It had two laboratory classrooms and a lecture hall, a student infirmary, date rooms and recreational spaces. We could sunbathe on the roof.

On September 4, "Today I began my profession of nursing." It was the first day of nursing school for 56 of us probies. We became known as the Class of '59 of the Touro Infirmary School of Nursing, given the acronym of TISON by a classmate, Nadine Lott, who did not actually graduate.

During my tenure, September 4, 1956-September 3, 1959, at Touro Infirmary, Miss Althea Dopp, a Touro graduate, was the Director of Nursing and Miss Annie Louise Thorpe, a registered nurse but not a Touro graduate, was the Director of Nursing Education.

## Homesick

Arriving at a new place
bombarded by
homesickness

It was only 280 miles from Vaiden, but I felt I had traveled far from home. It might as well have been a continent away. It felt like it to me. Indeed, it was a world removed from my roots. I knew nothing about the city, the people, the school or what to expect.

True I was on an adventure and very busy, but my homesickness for my family and my small town of Vaiden was pronounced. But no one doubted my seriousness, and I was never in doubt that my dream and prayer to become a nurse wouldn't come true. I missed everyone and everything, my mother, my grandmother, my siblings, my town, my friends. It was a package deal, all in one. If I had anyone of these with me, even then I would have been homesick.

Oh gosh, as I sit here and recall that September day, when in the years before I would have been set for the new school year at Vaiden High School, I was in New Orleans with the unknown ahead of me.

I was not the only one in the dormitory who was homesick, and we talked about our homesickness by the hour. Tears flowed. One friend, June Brock, told a tall tale about me climbing under one of our beds to weep. That was a tall tale, but it was her perception. We couldn't even get under our beds, which were less than six inches from the floor, unless we first turned into a pancake.

But I do stand accused of being sick for my home and the people I left behind. I must have looked pitiful. On July 31, 2000, while attending a small reunion with some nursing school classmates in Surf City, New Jersey, another classmate, Connie Thomas Miller, again repeated June's exaggeration of the truth.

My brief diary notes demonstrate my acute homesickness. You can also see the conflict within me by my diary entries. It took months, if not years, to adjust to my changed world. September 5, 1956: "Classes are in progress now. Assigned four chapters in nursing arts. A little homesick." Two days later on September 7: "Had a rough day today. I was really homesick. We toured Tulane. Really thought about going home soon. 'Letter.' To whom that letter was written, I have no idea.

On September 10, "Still homesick. We had a student council meeting. Eating bills [Touro staff must have been telling us this, as we did not have to pay for our food] are too high. Lots of work to do."

My first trip home was for a short weekend. I was able to get a ride with Betty Cummins Clark. We left on Friday afternoon. There were no superhighways, no I-10 nor I-55, just plain old two lane highways, and it seemed like it took hours to get there. We arrived late at night according to my diary entry of October 5, "Came home. Got here about 1:30 Saturday morning. Marvin Cade—he is my three year old brother—in the hospital." I wrote on October 6, "At home. Went to Grenada Hospital. Talked to so many people. Had a good time." I had one day to spend with the family, and it was a full one.

All day long that day I was thinking, "By tomorrow this time, I'll be headed back to New Orleans." The train ran I heard the whistle; I thought to myself, "That's the last time I'll hear that train whistle for a long time." Every meal that I ate, I'd say to myself, "This is the last lunch, or last supper, I'll have with my family for a long time." But I did write on October 7, "Kind of glad to be back."

But at home with my family I never showed that misery. It never occurred to me to talk about my homesickness with my family. No one would have understood, and I wasn't accustomed to unburdening my misery on my family. Plus they may have told me to come on home, and that wasn't in my plan. After the two week holiday vacation to Vaiden over the Christmas1956 and New Year's holiday 1957, I wrote in my diary on January 7, 1957, "Got a depressing letter from Sarah Lou. Said they cried when I left home. I cried." Another diary entry March 11, 1957: "To Tulane-a letter from Daddy. Wants me to come home."

But not once did I think seriously of returning to Vaiden or leaving the nursing school. My homesickness did not hamper my focus. If anything, it gave me focus. But that sensation of homesickness did not just pass over night. It lingered and lingered like a flu virus. One day I would forget about it, and the next day it would raise its head again. But finally it went away like a wart sometimes disappears on your hand. You don't remember the day it left, but it is gone. The love you had for family, friends, and your little small town was still there, but you knew you would see them time and time again.

## Home Experience

I had commitment and self-discipline, and my home experience had taught me a lot first hand. My mother's parents and my grandmother's sister lived with us a few years before they died. Since Mama Mann and Cedy were bed bound, I was called to active nursing duty before I had the professional training to do so. While helping to care for them, I did not realize strategies for my future were developing.

If they were incontinent, I do not remember. Neither do I remember that either of them had bedsores, pneumonia, or other respiratory problems, yet neither of them ever got out of bed. My grandmother actually sat on the side of the bed all day and all night. In other words, my grandmother never took her feet off of the floor. She only complained when you tried to get her to put her feet on the bed.

## Roommates

However, nothing in my upbringing prepared me for the response to the freedom from the home environment that many girls demonstrated. My first roommate was Joel Lazarus. Our room number was 709.

The first week, Joel was ready to drink and party. I was ready to study and study more, to make new friends, to experience freedom with responsibility, and to get over my dreadful homesickness. Joel did not last a year. In my diary on January 3, 1957, I wrote that all of the students returned from the holiday vacation except Joel Lazarus, Patsy Fugler, and Carol McRee.

Joel and I were roommates for about one week. In my diary I wrote on September 10, 1956, "I went to church. Moved in a new roommate, Treva Ann Barlow, and was homesick." Treva and I got along well. She was smart and she did well, but she did not like the nursing experience. She managed to stay through the capping exercise. But on June 21 I wrote, "My roommate I think is leaving this time." She was not there when I returned from an overnight with Mina on June 22. On June 28 I wrote, "Treva came after her clothes." I missed Treva and we stayed in contact for years.

Despite my personal shock regarding an early roommate's behavior, Touro provided a safe place and nurturing environment for a young student nurse adjusting to leaving home.

## Big-Little Sisters, Housemothers, Behavior and Health Keepers

Big-Little Sister week began the first week of school. Upper class students adopted one of us and the first week or two we received notes and little surprise gifts appeared in our mail boxes signed "From your Big Sister." That was lots of fun, and I wrote in my diary on September 20, 1956, "Last day to live in suspense. I learned who my Big Sister is. She is Patsy Shepherd from Florida." One of the little gifts that she gave me I still have. It was a little bear piggy bank.

The end of that week we probationers were treated to an evening of refreshments and entertainment by the upper class students. My Little Sister the next year was Bernie Mellon.

We had a variety of people who were responsible for our physical and mental health and our "moral lives." We had lots of rules such as no visitor could go beyond first floor without permission and strict curfews which were intended to ensure that students were healthy and rested for their nursing duties.

We had "housemothers" who watched over us in the dorm and made sure that we followed those rules and curfews. Part of their responsibility was to see we followed the dormitory rules regarding the time when the lights were to be out.

Some housemothers were better than others at letting us know we had broken a rule. Others were more relaxed about the rules if no harm was done. Mrs. Annie Frank was our beloved night housemother, and many of us were fond of her. She often ignored the lights that some of us burned throughout the night before a major exam.

Our rooms were also subject to inspection by the housemothers, and we were expected to keep them neat and tidy. If a room was untidy or beds were unmade more than a certain number of times, there were consequences. A student might be referred to the Judiciary Council of the Student Council for infractions of the house rule

The Student Council had representatives of the student body elected as president, vice president, secretary, treasurer, each class president, the various chairmen—social, athletic, big sister, library and the nominating committee—and a faculty advisor. Social and recreational aspects of student life were the primary concerns of the Student Council.

The Judiciary Council was a subsection of the Student Council with a chairman elected by the student body, each class president, and an elected representative from each class. Infractions of rules were referred to the council, and those penalties usually were loss of time the students could be away from the dorm. During my Touro Infirmary years to be "on campus" was the most severe penalty given. If you were campused you were required to wear your uniform day and night except to sleep. Therefore, you could only go to and from the hospital to sleep and eat and otherwise you were confined to the dorm.

I remember being guilty of breaking one of those regulations prior to my senior year when I became more brazen. The rule that I broke, recorded in my diary in early January 1958, had to do with the Monday night expectation that we were to be in the dormitory by 7 P.M. I was in the home of a friend, Mina Windecker's sister-in-law, in Harahan, Louisiana, a suburb of New Orleans. Somehow I remembered it was Monday night and rushed back to the dorm, but it was too late. I had to go to the Judiciary Council and I knew some kind of penalty was in store. I was placed "on campus" for one week.

I remember that I spent lots of time in the library during that time. But that was like throwing Brer Rabbit into the briar patch; I gobbled it up. It would have taken a wedge to get me out of those books. One friend and fellow classmate accused me of reading the dictionary.

8/26/59

Dear Noah, S.M.,
    Here's to one of
the most individu-
alistic people I
know! You've really
added a bright
spot to these three
years! I don't think
I'll ever forget you,
Noah, and the moments
we shared. As long as
I live I'll never for-
get the night I saw
you reading the diction-
ary! Real typical!
    I love ya!
    Brownie.

159

Due to students staffing a large portion of the hospital, our health was a major concern. Our in-house physician was Dr. Maud Loeber, the daughter of Touro's first resident physician. Within the nurse's residence was an infirmary, and there was a full time registered nurse, Roberta McAnally, R.N., assigned to our physical health care needs. Miss Matlock was there to tend our social and mental health needs.

Touro provided a protective environment to keep us safe, something that many of us, including me, needed. I was too immature to understand some of the rules at the time, and perhaps I thought I was wise enough to set my own limits.

## Small Town Mississippi compared to New Orleans

Not enough can be said about the "City Shock" that I felt. Until I was 15 years old, I had lived in the small community of Blackmonton in Carroll County, Mississippi, about ten miles outside the city limits of Vaiden. In the country our nearest neighbor was at least a half a mile away. In New Orleans the houses were so close together that if one spoke real loud the neighbor could hear the latest gossip or other personal things. There were no air conditioners with compressors to hinder hearing the private matters of neighbors in the 1950s and earlier times.

The entire experience—nursing school, the city, the culture, the music, the food, the history—was one gigantic adventure and learning experience for me. New Orleans was a Southern city in latitude, but most of the population did not speak Southern. I spoke Southern then, and 48 years later, I speak Southern. It is said that New Orleans is in the South, but not of the South.

In one section of New Orleans, especially what is known as the 9th ward, there was and still is a unique way of saying certain words like mynaze for mayonnaise, zinc for sink, silver dime, making groceries, gallery for porch, banquette for sidewalk, erl for oil.

I had to learn to pronounce many of the patients' surnames and fellow students' names. Some common names in this part of the country were very uncommon to me like, Boudreaux (pronounced Boo-drow with a long o for the drow), Hebert (pronounced A bear), Thibodaux (pronounced Tib [like bib]-i-dough), Richard (pronounced Ree-chard not Rich-ard), Theriot (pronounced Terry-o), and many more.

160

I was living in a dormitory with about 100 girls from diverse backgrounds, well-off and poor, from multiple states, large cities and small towns, and from various religious backgrounds including Protestant, Catholic, and Jewish.

I grew up in the part of the South where the dominant belief system was Protestant. I was a Presbyterian and had known many Baptists, and Methodists. I saw little difference except in our baptism methods. The Methodists and Presbyterians sprinkled water on the head of the one being baptized, usually as an infant or young child, while the Baptist submerged the one being baptized. You could become a Presbyterian or Methodist without being re-baptized while in order to become a Baptist, you had to first be submerged.

We also came in contact with an occasional Jehovah's Witness and maybe a Mormon from time to time. Also, I had known a few people who were called Holy Rollers, but I had never attended their services so only knew second hand that Holy Rollers got extremely emotional in their religious response.

But I had come to Touro Infirmary, a hospital established by Jewish people, with many Jewish doctors and administrators. I knew about Jewish people from Sunday School and the Bible, but I had never met a Jewish person. If I had, I didn't know it, and in my school and town I knew everyone. Everyone was associated with a church in some fashion, and I knew which protestant church they belonged to. If not a Protestant, then I knew they were either a Jehovah's Witness or Mormon.

My great Aunt Lou was Catholic. She was a devoted Christian, a devoted wife, and a wonderful person. I only knew she used prayer beads, although I never heard her say a Hail Mary, and I knew that she had to go to Winona, ten miles from Vaiden, to attend mass. Much later I learned that in New Orleans I was living in a sea of Catholics.

Judah Touro, who left money for the founding of Touro and in whose honor Touro Infirmary is named, would have been proud of the ecumenical spirit at Touro Infirmary. There were Jewish doctors, Jewish nurses, and Jewish administrators. There were Jewish holidays: Yom Kippur, Purim, Hanukkah, Passover, and Rosh Hashanah set aside for folks of the Jewish faith.

But Christmas holidays were celebrated also. We had a Christmas Dance, Christmas trees in the dorm and on the hospital units, and we had Santa Claus.

One of the highlights of our social calendar was the Christmas Dance held each year at a hotel. In 1958 it was held in the Coker Room of the Municipal Auditorium. The Christmas Dance had a queen selected by the student body, along with maids representing each class. In my senior year I was elected the class maid and Madeline Gallagher was the queen. When the first vote for class maid was taken, Ann Brownell and I had tied. Another vote was taken and I won. Though I was her opponent, Ann offered to let me wear her beautiful evening gown, and I took her up on her offer. She was a special person then and has remained so.

My date for the event was Milton McCuskey, a medical student at Tulane. I do not remember how I met Milton, but I recorded on October 18, 1958, "Out with Milton to AKK [that's a medical fraternity] party and to the French Quarter afterward." The next day I recorded, "To church with Milton." I should have been impressed with him taking me to church, but I wasn't then and never was, though I must admit he was a nice person. I do know that he later interned in Montreal, and after that internship he returned to Tulane for an internal medicine residency. One day during anesthesia he came down to the delivery room area and we talked but we never got together again.

There were opportunities to observe Jewish rituals and ceremonies such as the bris (circumcision). Friends of the Jewish faith invited me to attend Friday night services at the Touro Synagogue.

Under these conditions, I learned that Jews, Catholics and Protestants can live in close quarters, get along, and learn to respect each other, to love one another, to share, to hope and to learn.

I also learned the value of being ecumenical, and I practiced it. My diary entry on April 5, 1957: "To temple." I believe I went to the Touro Synagogue with my classmate Sharon Singerman who later married a Lutheran and became a converted Christian. On April 21, 1957, I wrote: "To church with Margaret." Margaret was Methodist. On April 20, 1958, I wrote: "To mass with Mina." On December 24, 1957: "Mrs. Joachim (a housemother) and I are going to midnight mass tonight." January 5, 1958, "June and I went to First Baptist Church. Pat Ashley brought us home."

Touro Infirmary School of Nursing

Requests the pleasure of your company

at

The Christmas Dance

on Thursday, December the eleventh

at nine o'clock

Coker Room

Municipal Auditorium

1958

Touro Infirmary School of Nursing Christmas Court Dec. 1958
Fifth couple from the right Milton McCuskey and Carolyn Noah

The weather seemed more unpredictable. New Orleans was a lot warmer in the winter than Vaiden, although on February 12, 1958, I wrote in my diary, "Snowed in New Orleans, Louisiana. Phi Chi Fraternity guys came over and we had fun. Miss Thorpe came out to see what was happening." However, many times I did not need a coat in the wintertime. But the summer heat could be breathtaking.

On June 27, 1957, I gained a respect for hurricanes. I had heard about hurricanes from my aunt, Verna Mann Duke, who lived in Gulfport, Mississippi for many years, but I didn't process the meaning of what it meant weather wise. However, that June day a hurricane named Audrey hurled a raging ocean of water over Cameron Parish, Louisiana. It was a category four hurricane and in a few hours it wiped out every movable object in its path, forever changing the lives of those Cameron Parish folks and making an indelible impression upon me and leaving a respect for hurricanes forever. Hurricane Audrey killed 425 people, many of them a very young age.

There were colleges and universities galore in New Orleans. Tulane, Loyola, Xavier, Dillard, St. Mary's Dominican are those that come to mind, and there were more hospitals than universities. Vaiden had one small medical clinic with a solo general practice doctor. If we needed a hospital, we had to go to the next town ten miles away. Yet I can recall so many hospitals in this great city in 1956, including Touro Infirmary; Flint Goodrich, an all Black hospital at that time; Baptist; Mercy; Hotel Dieu; Sarah Mayo; Veterans; DePaul Psychiatric Hospital; St. Claude General; U.S. Public Health Hospital; Charity; and perhaps others that I do not recall.

Until I left that small town to come to New Orleans, I had been out of the state of Mississippi only twice. The first time was on my high school senior trip that took our class to Alabama and Florida. The only other time was the brief trek to Cicero, Illinois that I mentioned earlier. And now I was in New Orleans, the sixteenth largest city in the United States in the 1950 census. Vaiden had a population of less than a thousand. Touro Infirmary staff, patients, and student nurses alone almost equaled the population of my hometown.

In Vaiden one could walk from one side of the town to the other in 30-45 minutes. Since there was no Crescent City Connection to connect the East and West banks of New Orleans in 1956, the ferry was the only way to get from downtown New Orleans to the West Bank. The notorious

Governor Huey P. Long, who had had no love for New Orleans, had the Huey Long Bridge built farther upriver to connect the East and West Banks of Jefferson Parish.

Lake Pontchartrain, which cradles the northern shore of New Orleans, provides a recreational area for the locals, and during my nursing school years, the Pontchartrain Beach Amusement Park was a wonderful place to go. I rode my first roller coaster, the Zephyr, at Pontchartrain Beach.

New Orleans had streetcars, public buses, and taxis. There were buildings with multiple stories that had elevators and escalators. Our dormitory for student nurses had eight floors and a sunroof. From this sunroof you got a good view of a large part of the city. The city was aglow at nighttime from the rooftop, and I developed passion aplenty for this nighttime view. In Vaiden there were no buildings with more than two stories.

In New Orleans, people had locks on their doors and even in the dorm we girls each had a key to our room. I had never lived in a house that had a lock on a door, and I had never had to keep up with a key in my life. A big city it was and a small town country girl had come to the city.

In 1956 a nine-year-old could buy hard liquor at the grocery store in New Orleans. This was a hard-drinking town. At the time this seemed outrageous to me, and my mother would have been mortified. I did know my maternal grandmother liked to drink bootleg whiskey, but I had surely not seen my mother drink anything stronger than a RC Cola. Years later when I talked to her about these early experiences, Mother said to me that she was glad that I was the one who came to New Orleans and not my sister. Mother said she didn't think my sister would have lived through young adulthood in New Orleans with the kinds of experiences that I had.

The French Quarter, also called the Vieux Carre, is the earliest part of New Orleans. It is what many thought then and think of now as the whole of New Orleans, but is indeed only a small ten square block area of the City of New Orleans. I do love the French Quarter and lived there a short while after nursing school graduation, but there's so much more to this great exotic city.

My mother called New Orleans the "Sin City." Why she thought that I do not know, and where she got her information was a question that comes to me. Mother had never been out of the state of Mississippi until she was over 40, and we didn't have all of this worldly news that we have on radio and television today. She'd certainly never been to New Orleans. I continue to wonder.

The cemeteries were different, too. Nowadays we call them "Cities of the Dead." Most of the graves are above ground, and a tomb is a family tomb. A year and a day after a family member passes, when another family member dies, that family member can be buried in the same tomb. People all over the city place flowers on graves for All Saints Day, which is November 1. I was accustomed to placing flowers on graves, too, but at a different time. I don't think I had ever heard of All Saints Day.

There were new and different music sounds. I sang church hymns, heard plenty of country music and some popular music. I knew about Elvis Presley and rock and roll in my youth. I had heard and enjoyed some spiritual music in Black churches. I knew patriotic songs and I sang songs from the Broadway show, "Showboat," in the school glee club. What I didn't know about was jazz with its unique rhythm and the blues. I was now living in New Orleans, the birthplace of jazz. Perhaps I should have known about the blues, but I didn't.

Oh, the food! One could find the Mississippi food, the turnip greens, black-eyed peas, and cornbread that I was accustomed to eating at home, but sometimes it was not easy. What I came to know in New Orleans was the Creole French, the continental French, and the Italian food. It was a culinary heaven with filé gumbo, crawfish etouffé, and jambalaya. It took me a long while to learn to eat raw oysters and to eat the boiled shrimp and crawfish spread out on newspaper on a table.

There were McKenzie's, doughnuts but the more popular doughnuts, especially for the tourists and newcomers like me, were the beignets which were served with café au lait (equal parts of coffee, usually with chicory and whole milk). At Café du Monde in the French Quarter the beignets were covered with powdered sugar that got all over you and the surrounding party, too.

## Mardi Gras

Mardi Gras, imbedded into the culture of New Orleans and called the Greatest Free Show on Earth, was an event I had heard of prior to coming to New Orleans, but never did I have a description of the biggest event on the calendar in New Orleans when the city did not sleep for twenty-four hours.

On the sixth day of January, sometimes called Little Christmas, sometimes Twelfth Night, and sometimes King's Day, we were able to buy the first king cakes at McKenzie's Bakery. Other bakeries also may have made them, but I only knew about McKenzie's then. King cakes have changed over time, but in those days they were round or rectangular pastries with purple, gold, and green granulated sugar on top. Inside was a small plastic baby doll, and whoever got the piece of cake with the baby was to provide the next king cake. For me, the arrival of the king cake meant the beginning of Mardi Gras. I learned later that Mardi Gras preparations were actually year-round, though not all of the hoopla.

Generally the parades would begin on a week-end about two weeks prior to Mardi Gras Day, also called Fat Tuesday and Shrove Tuesday. Ash Wednesday, first day of Lent, was the day following Mardi Gras, and part of the catholic religious custom was to go to a catholic church and get ashes placed on one's forehead by the priest. For Catholics, Lent was a time of penitence until Easter arrived.

Natives knew to either take part in the holiday, stay at home, or to leave town for Mardi Gras Day or for the season. Officially, the season begins on the sixth of January, called Twelfth Night, when the first Carnival ball is held. There are balls up to and including Mardi Gras night. As student nurses at Touro, we participated in the Mardi Gras. My first Mardi Gras experience was a parade. On February 24, 1957, I wrote, "Went to see Mina and went to parade." It was on Tulane Avenue a few blocks from Mina's home. The parades were fairly well orchestrated and the parade had a delineated route that was published in the newspaper so the parade-goers could line up along the route. Most of the parade consisted of elaborate paper mache floats pulled by tractors with masked people on them who belonged to a Krewe.

Along the route were throngs of people, parents, children, grandparents, and friends, on the sidewalk side or the neutral ground side. In New Orleans the median is called a neutral ground supposedly because it was a neutral zone to separate the French settlers from the newly arriving American immigrants. The revelers would be standing on their tiptoes along the route, waving and thrashing their hands as if reaching to the heavens and calling out anthem-like, "Throw me something, Mister" or with that special New Orleans pronunciation, "Trow me sumtin, mistuh!" The maskers on the floats were being beckoned to toss cheap, though much cherished glass beads, and the spectators wanted to catch as many beads as they could, even though they would end up in some box the next day after Mardi Gras, Ash Wednesday.

There were marching bands in between the floats. That kept the noise of the revelers quiet. The next float would come along and everyone would again stand on their tiptoes, waving and thrashing their hands saying and yelling that familiar refrain, "Throw me something, Mister." Those words became infectious. By the time the second float passed, at my first parade, I was imitating the other spectators.

During parade times, main street routes were blocked for hours. In my early experience in the city, I never thought how one would react to an emergency. I suppose if a baby was coming, if there was a serious automobile accident, or some other kind of emergency, some route would have to be found to get to a hospital. But it looked like to me that the world had stopped.

That same year on March 2, 1957, I wrote "to a Masquerade Party." I was invited party by Betty Cummins Clark, one of the two Touro graduates from Vaiden mentioned earlier in this legacy.

This was my initiation to New Orleans parties and the expectation that drinking mixed drinks was the "in thing" to do, and if you didn't do so, you were out. I had never even heard of mixed drinks, my dad drank home-made bootleg whiskey straight. I didn't dare ask what was in the drinks, and in order to seem like I knew what was going on, I pointed to a drink someone else had and said, "I'll take what she has." I had no idea what it was, but with my first sip, I knew I didn't like it. I think it was bourbon and Coke, and as soon as I could, I went to the bathroom and disposed of it.

My diary entry of February 18, 1958, brings another drinking experience to mind. "Mardi Gras Day. To Pat O'Brien's. First time. Drank one Tom Collins. The two people who I recall being there with me were my classmate, Connie Thomas, and her friend, Robert Cornet, a Tulane football player from Connie's home town of Hattiesburg, Mississippi.

## Other Drinking Experiences

My drinking experiences continued to be few and far between. I kept track of them for the first two years. Sometime prior to April 6, 1958, I had asked Fred Wulff, a Tulane student, to attend the Junior-Senior Prom at Touro with me. I had met Fred either in Sunday School at the

St. Charles Avenue Presbyterian Church or at the Westminster Fellowship House, a Presbyterian-sponsored meeting place, on Broadway near the Tulane/Newcomb Campus.

My diary note on Easter Sunday April 6, 1958, was "To W.F. [this meant Westminster Fellowship] Easter Sunday, a very pretty day. Fred coming to prom." Asking Fred to prom was a big deal for me, as I had never asked a guy for a date or invited a guy to any kind of event in my entire life. If he had said no, it would have been my first and last time to invite any guy to go any place with me. From that experience I gained some insight into how guys may have felt if they asked someone for a date and were turned down.

Fred made my third liquor drinking experience funny, memorable and pleasurable. At the junior-senior prom on April 10, 1958, I wrote "Night of junior-senior prom. Had a good time."

Fred did not ask me what I wanted to drink. He took it upon himself to order for me. He ordered half Coke and half Seven-Up. This guy knew my type, and he was a New Orleanian. I do not know whatever happened to Fred. He was in the ROTC, I think the Marines, at Tulane. After finishing Tulane, he went to Quantico, Virginia, for some kind of Marine training experience. I saw him once afterward, but did not keep in touch.

My fourth drinking experience is not recorded. However, in my memory it is indelible. Toward the end of my senior year, I had metamorphosed a bit, took a chance, broke a rule, went out with two friends and classmates, June Brock and Connie Thomas, to Schwegmann's on Airline Highway and bought a bottle of port wine.

On the way back to the dorm, we stopped at June's brother Gene's apartment and I guzzled the port. We all returned to the dorm. Mrs. Frank was the housemother on duty, thank goodness. I was very drunk, barely able to stand up, but managed to stagger into the dorm. Mrs. Frank automatically placed my room key on top of the desk. She may or may not have noticed my condition. Friends picked up my key for me and took me to my room. I went to bed, slept it off, and arose the next morning and went to work, never missing a beat. I didn't have a hangover then, and have never had one since. However, I learned a lesson for a lifetime, and perhaps I have never lost control in such a precarious way ever again.

## Other Social Experiences

There were many social opportunities and activities that we engaged in though we were an all-female student body. I recorded some of them.

October 16, 1956, "Played first volley ball game and lost."

October 19: "Tonight I played ping pong with June Brock."

December 7, 1957: "June Brock and I went to an orphanage."

December 16, 1957, "Had Christmas banquet. I told Benny that it began at eight instead of seven, and boy was I upset when I could not get him. He came." Benny Ferdon was a Tulane student who also attended Presbyterian activities. Later he was in Tulane Medical School with my longtime boyfriend, Henry Giles.

We also had places in the neighborhood where we liked to hang out. Allgoods, a neighborhood restaurant, was located across from the hospital, and we often went there to have long discussions with fellow students and the residents and interns.

The Women's Auxiliary of Touro Infirmary took on some of the responsibility for providing some of our social and recreational activities. From them we received free tickets to the New Orleans Symphony and opera and to the Pops concerts.

## Other diary recordings

There were trips home to Vaiden, letters from family and friends, and visits from family and friends.

November 12, 1957: "Daddy called me. Got a letter from Daddy today. Aunt Lou, Big Bud and Daddy are coming down this weekend."

November 15: "Daddy, Aunt Lou, and Big Bud are here. I went to see them."

November 26, 1957: "To Sister's tomorrow."

November 28: "Thanksgiving Day in Gulfport. Sister, Janice and I went to a football game—Gulfport and Biloxi."

## Tulane Experience

Soon after enrolling in the School of Nursing at Touro Infirmary, we began classes at Tulane University, where we took basic science courses in chemistry, anatomy and physiology, microbiology, psychology, and sociology. We also took a semester of English at Tulane. None of us had cars, so to get to Tulane we took public transportation. Depending on the class location at Tulane, we either rode the Freret Street bus or the St. Charles Avenue streetcar, which cost us seven cents.

On September 13 I wrote, "The nursing class of 1959 registered at Tulane today." We went in the mornings or afternoons to class at Tulane three times a week for one academic year.

On October 3, 1956, I recorded "Went to Tulane. Made A on chemistry. Am still studying hard." I always did study hard every day, as I was not good at the heroic crams that some of my classmates performed well. Plus I had an unwavering determination to excel. It was years later when I read that Thomas Edison said, "Genius is one percent inspiration and ninety-nine percent perspiration." I was insightful enough to grasp that prior to going to nursing school.

Not everyone was doing well. On January 12, 2002, Shirley Griffin Norman, former classmate, who was in our class through capping, but left soon afterward, gave this account of one of her chemistry experiments. "We were doing a chemistry lab experiment, and I knew I would not be able to do it. The female professor told us not to taste of the outcome of the test, otherwise it might kill us. I worked and worked. I thought it was salt. I didn't care if I died. I tasted it anyway."

On that same day Shirley shared another chemistry anecdote. "I stayed up all night cramming for the chemistry test. During the test I realized I had my notes open on top of my chemistry book. Knowing we were on the honor system, I thought I had better 'fess up' and went up to tell the professor about my open notes." The professor told her, "Honey, I know by your grades you didn't cheat."

I never really knew why Shirley left, as she seemed to love nursing. Shirley told me she should never have been allowed to enter nursing as she felt poorly prepared by her small town Mississippi school experience. We had a great laugh when Shirley told of her problems with pharmacology. Indisputably, I was flabbergasted when she said to me, "I have never met anyone who came up to the standards of those nursing school classmates of mine. I was mesmerized."

My success continued.

On October 8: "Another Tulane day. Had an anatomy test. Made a C. Wear uniform tomorrow."

October 15: "I went to Tulane. Made a 100 on an anatomy test. Seems like a miracle."

October 22: "This has been a good day. In anatomy and physiology we dissected a rat. It was funny. Made a 100 on anatomy."

On October 29: "Went to Tulane. Worked with human arms and legs. Made a 93 on a test."

December 3: "Went to Tulane. Studied brain of a sheep. Made 86 on test."

On January 21, 1957: "An anatomy and physiology exam. Study for chemistry."

January 22: "English and chemistry exam." We had now finished the first semester at Tulane.

On January 29 1957, "To Tulane to register again. Went to see Aunt Lou afterwards."

February 5, 1957: "First classes here second semester."

On February 6, 1957, I wrote. "To Tulane. Looked through a microscope."

I did not record much about my second semester Tulane experience. I usually just put "To Tulane" without any explanation, although I did record on May 20, "sociology exam" and on May 21, 1957, "microbiology exam." Then, on May 23, "Six failed microbiology. Billie failed psychology."

## Learning to Practice Nursing

In addition to our Tulane classes, there was no postponing the real reason we were at Touro Infirmary. We were in training to become bedside nurses. Nursing arts classes began the first week of school. The term came from Sir William Osler who said the concept of nursing is "an art to be cultivated as a profession."

Before going to the hospital wards we were all issued a uniform to be worn on the hospital units. It was a multiple-piece uniform. The pre-clinicals or probies, as we were called wore a blue checkered dress with a starched, gored apron without a bib. That dress and apron came almost to our ankles. This apron overlapped in the back and was held tightly to our waist with two buttons. Our bandage scissors were placed between these buttons, making them readily available without the need for disarraying the apron to root for the scissors in the uniform pocket.

Starched cuffs were attached to the sleeves, and we wore a Buster Brown collar around our neck. We wore white stockings with white oxford shoes. After the capping exercise, we added an apron, bib, and the cap to our uniform.

In the winter, a wool cape was part of the uniform. It was navy blue and "Touro" was written on the collar.

The dress code required that our hair could not be longer than shoulder length unless we wore it up in a bun. We could wear no jewelry other than a wrist watch. Prior to going to the wards, we had trial periods in the laboratory. On September 6, 1956, I wrote "First day in laboratory. Changed bed and went through procedure. A letter from Sarah Lou."

September 11: "In lab I bathed a patient."

On September 12: "I was given a bed bath."

On September 13: "I gave a bed bath."

It was just over one month after arriving at Touro Infirmary that we probies were scattered around the various hospital wards to practice on real live patients the procedures that we had learned in the classroom. There was always an instructor hovering nearby so that we followed proper procedure and to make sure no patients were at risk. My diary entry on October 11 was. "First day on ward. Top it all, I had to bathe a 29-year-old man. Gee, I was nervous."

In the early days of our first year, what we could do was limited, but we had one thing that counted for a lot, and that was enthusiasm. There weren't any problems identifying us from the upper class students. We stood out with our checkered dresses, long starched aprons without the bibs, white stockings, and no caps. The patients loved the wide-eyed, if a little scared and anxious, very professional first year student nurses.

A fellow classmate, Barbara Byrd, later Rome, shared an early probie experience with me. "When I was still a 'probie' I was on one of the female charity units. A patient was having diarrhea and I went into the hopper room to clean her dirty drawers. I then flushed one of only two pair of drawers this poor woman had down the hopper. I remember the horror of those pants going down the pipe. Later I went to Magazine Street, bought her some more drawers, and sneaked them into the lady's cubicle."

Every week we learned a new procedure, usually preceded by classroom discussion and a practice session on Miss Chase, the mannequin. Our follow through was on the units where were practiced on a real live person, with that ever-present instructor nearby.

On each of the wards there was a standard procedure book. A record was kept on each of us, and we had to demonstrate proficiency to be signed off on each procedure.

One of the first procedures we learned was giving enemas. There were some patients who stayed in the hospital months, if not years, unlike today, and if that patient had constipation, many of us demonstrated this procedure on him or her. On February 11, 1957, I wrote, "Catheterization done. To Tulane."

## Injection Experiences

We all undoubtedly have some kind of recall regarding our first injection. As with most of what we learned, our instructors first explained the procedure to us. We then had our laboratory practice.

We did not practice on each other, but practiced giving shots using oranges. Miss Chase did not get any injections because she would have deteriorated rapidly.

We learned that first we had to prepare the patient by explaining the procedure, one of the constants in the medical arena. For an intramuscular injection, we had the patient to turn on the side to expose the upper outer quadrant of the buttock. We cleaned the area with a cotton ball soaked with alcohol. The needle and syringe were held about two inches from the site where we hoped to inject the medication. When we were ready to inject the patient, we took the injection and we aimed it at the proper area using a wrist motion.

In the 1950s we were not yet using disposable needles. The needles were autoclaved and used over and over. Consequently, some of the needles had burrs on them and did not go in so easily, making the procedure more painful for both the patient and the nurse.

For June 18, my diary says, "First day on meds. First I.M." I remember explaining to the patient that I was going to give him an injection, but didn't tell him it was my first one. When I asked him to turn on his side, he turned so that his right buttock was up. I cleaned the surface with alcohol and then stuck him. He started out on one side of the bed and swiftly moved to the other side. I was glad the side rail was up; otherwise the patient would have been on the floor.

On June 19 I wrote, "Felt horrible. Better on shots. G.I. hour exam."

Sue Livingston (Benning), originally from Cleveland, Mississippi, gave me this personal account of her first injection. "I could hardly sleep that night. The next morning I was scheduled to give my first injection to some poor soul. We had only practiced on oranges. Would I really be able to puncture someone's skin with a needle?

"There were too many things to remember. I had to select a perfect place in the upper outer flank, cleanse the area with an alcohol wipe, stick the needle in quickly and smoothly, pull the barrel to see if I had hit a vein by accident, then push the needle in! After this was accomplished, I was supposed to withdraw the needle quickly and press the alcohol wipe on the spot. Oh brother, that poor patient! I was a nervous wreck! I could just see me holding that shaky syringe!

"I arrived early on the ward to see one of the male patients pacing up and down the floor. Later, I was told his name was Mr. Cutler. I was informed that he was the patient my instructor, Miss Hill, had selected for me to do the deed. He had given his permission for an unknown student nurse to practice on him. (Was he insane?) He obviously was nervous; he was still pacing the floor.

"Miss Hill performed the introductions and explained that she would be there to supervise. We went into his room, and he pulled his pajamas down. Miss Hill suggested he lie down and turn on his side. (Did she think I was going to be that bad?

"I cleansed the area, drew back the syringe and moved it forward. It barely touched his skin. He jumped. I barely muffled a scream! I was never going to be able to do this.

"Miss Hill ushered me out of the room, explaining to Mr. Cutler that we would return, if that was okay with him.

"She calmly steered me into the nourishment room, and selected an orange from the refrigerator. We practiced, I guess too long, for Mr. Cutler found us just as I was thrusting the needle into the orange. His eyes got big, and his face turned white! Miss Hill asked him if he still wanted to volunteer and he gave a weak yes. I <u>had</u> to put this man out of his misery!

I prayed all the way to his room, promised God I would go back to church, and do anything he wanted if I could just learn to 'do shots'.

Mr. Cutler held tightly to the bed and closed his eyes (He was probably praying also), and I DID IT! I actually performed, under pressure. Mr.

Cutler didn't move. I thought he was dying. But Miss Hill assured me he was just as relieved that it was over."

"So there you have it. The story of my 'First Shot'. Just one of the many fascinating incidents that really happened to the student nurses at Touro."

Only Sue could remember such details.

Sue wrote in my yearbook.

DEAR NOAH,
    YOU'RE A WONDERFUL GIRL AND FRIEND. I GUESS
YOU'RE AMONG THE FEW WHOLESOME GIRLS IN THIS
OLE WORLD. THANKS FOR BEING THE WAY YOU ARE,
IT HELPED A WHOLE LOT IN THESE PAST YEARS.
THE BEST OF LUCK AND HAPPINESS. I'D LIKE TO
SAY MORE, ESPECIALLY BESIDES THESE ROUTINE THINGS,
BUT, IF IT HELPS, ANY. I MEAN THEM. COME SEE
US.
                        Love you
                        Sue

## Still Other Experiences

We learned various other procedures and many were documented in my diary. On July 10, 1957, I wrote, "Care for the dead. A letter from mother, said Sidney [he's my first cousin] ran in a ditch was unconscious and man found him." On July 17 I wrote, "On O2. Venous pressure. Signed off pre-op."

Our days were full of adventure, yes, but our instructors were serious. We were there for learning the best patient care. The patient and the patient's needs were the reason for this early clinical experience. That was drilled into us, and I still know and believe it. For without the patient we wouldn't need the doctors, nurses, maintenance, dietary, or marketing personnel. We wouldn't even need hospitals, insurance companies, or DME companies. Then and now I see nurses, doctors, management, and employees in all departments as collaborators, not as adversaries.

**Touro Infirmary School of Nursing Capping Exercise June 3, 1957**

## Capping

After about nine months of study and practice, we were given some freedom and independence. My May 27, 1957, diary entry said, "First day on O2 [this was the clinic male ward] to be alone without instructor." By June 3, 1957, 31 of the original 56 of our class members reached a milestone. I wrote, "Capping night, Mama [my maternal grandmother], Aunt Lou, Mina, Fred, and Toni came."

At the capping ceremony we sang the Alma Mater.

Lend your ears, oh friends and loved ones
To this song of praise;
And your voices, hearts and spirits
Swell to height it lays
To thy noble Alma, Mater
Pay homage due.
Join with ours your laud and honor,
In this tribute true.
Girded with thy truth and mercy lift our eyes above.
To your call our hearts beat loyal,
In thy name we grow.
Alma Mater, Touro Infirmary,
May thy fame still glow

## Class Blocks

The day after we were capped, we were placed in blocks. A block usually consisted of six students, and we generally rotated together throughout the hospital. In my block were June Brock, Ann Rex, Sharon Singerman, LaRue Storey, Connie Thomas, and I. We were together so much of the time. Connie Thomas and I were sometimes known as the Bobbsey twins. Other classmates in this block became some of my very best friends during nursing school and have remained so today, 48 years later.

We were together for obstetrics, pediatrics, psychiatry, night duty, evening duty, and medical-surgical units, and surgery.

Some of our classmates could not recall blocks in the summer of 2000. I figured out why. The students in my block all remained from day one through graduation, whereas in many of the other blocks, many of the students quit or were kicked out prior to graduation.

I wrote on Sunday, June 16, 1957, "First Sunday to work." In other words, our weekends had been free until this point in our training. We were not "in utero" any longer. Working and attending classes could sometimes be grueling, but it was expected. We rarely missed classes or work assignments Some met the challenge and some did not.

## Doctor Respect

Part of what we understood in a diploma nursing school was great respect for the doctors. That was true for the staff doctors, for the residents, and for the interns. If one walked onto the unit and the nurses were seated, we automatically stood up. This became a reflex reaction for most of us. Over 40 years later, I continue to have that acquired reflex.

From early times, the philosophy that shaped the school's expectations of student nurses was summed up in an address given Dr. Isidore Cohn to the graduating class of 1936. "A nurse should be silent, swift, safe, smiling and solemn."

Silent of tongue
Swift in action
Safe in judgment
Smiling in countenance and
Solemn in devotion to duty.

Though this speech was given 20 years before my tenure at TISON, this philosophy had not changed.

It was a given that some doctors had fits. They could be mean to nurses, and it was understood that nurses never fought back. I recorded those types of experiences, too. July 19, 1957, "First time doctor blessed me out." I did not elaborate.

But another part of my diary that same day. "Spinal tap."

September 12: "Dr. W. Rosen really blessed me out." I was assigned to the Emergency Room at the time, so it can be assumed that this "blessing" occurred there.

## Home Again

It was now time for a two-week vacation. We had a month's vacation each year, but we first year students had already had two of the weeks at Christmas. We all did not go on vacations at the same time because we student nurses were counted on to staff many of the units, so the hospital would not have shut down. I was off from July 29 through August 12, 1957.

During those two weeks at home I continued diary documentation. On August 1, I wrote, "At home all day. Sarah Lou kept telling me I'd changed. I hope for the best if so." August 3: I wrote. "Lucretia and I went to Winona to meet Josephine. Josephine didn't come." Lucretia was a high school classmate, a fellow Presbyterian, and at the time a student at Mississippi Southern, now known as the University of Southern Mississippi in Hattiesburg, Mississippi.

August 4: "To church and Sunday School. Met the new preacher. Lucretia and I went to Westminster Fellowship. Sarah Lou went to Ruth Ann's. Daddy went to church."

August 5: "Lucretia called. Wanted me to come out and watch TV. I went. Put my uniform on. Looks natural."

August 8: "Spent the day with Ruby. Picked peas. Mother, Sarah Lou, and I shelled them tonight."

Finally, on August 9 I wrote, "Spent the night with Mama. Milked her cow." This must have been the last cow I ever milked.

By August 12, I was back in New Orleans. I wrote. "Back down here today. Glad to be back a little." Perhaps I was experiencing a lot less homesickness.

## Other Recorded Experiences

Other recorded experiences in my diary. On September 10, 1957, I wrote. "My first day in the emergency room." Miss Frazier was the Head Nurse. September 19 I wrote. "I am a member of Special Committee of Louisiana Student Nurses. Had a meeting today."

In the late 50's student nurses were still covering units on the 3-11 PM shifts and the 11 PM—7AM shifts. We were assigned to the various units throughout the hospital and we were placed in charge.

Touro in those days had special units set aside for the clinic patients. 02 was the male clinic ward and F2 was the female clinic ward. The patients on these units did not have private doctors, but were taken care of by the intern and residents.

I recorded on September 21, 1957, "First time on 3-11." My assignment was to O2, the male clinic ward. I was the charge nurse. I took the reports made assignments, and did any and everything that needed to be done. I remember that a black licensed practical nurse named Platt was my helper. She didn't seem very energetic, and I would have to push her to get her to do things that needed to be done. I was, and still am, always energetic and thought every nurse should be. Platt was not a bad person nor was she mean to me, and it must have been especially hard for her to be told what to do by an 18 year old student nurse. She had experience that I lacked, but I was in charge of her and the rest of the staff on the unit. There was a house supervisor and our instructor who could be called upon, however.

It was a time when hospitals mixed medical and surgical patients on the same unit. Some were acutely ill while others might be there for tests only. The nurse would have to prepare the patient for the next day's test. For instance, a patient who was to have a barium enema x-ray had to have enemas until clear and a large dose of castor oil.

I cringed when I gave the castor oil as I had memories of castor oil being one of the punishments meted out to us by Daddy if we ate green plums.

Other patients were first day post-operative, and others were there to go to surgery the next day. The medical patients had a variety of diagnoses including congestive heart failure, diabetes, and various cancers.

Miss Colomb was our student nurse instructor on the evening shift. She had this wonderful sense of humor and didn't take life so seriously. She was loved by many members of the student body.

However, I took life and the task at hand very seriously. What I remember about this experience is scanty, but I do remember that I knew each patient's diagnosis, all of their medications, the usual dosage, the use and potential side effect of each drug, and the use of each and every medication.

Two procedures that I remember are checking diabetic patients for their sugar levels prior to meals and starting of infusions. In order to check the sugar level, we had to have a specimen of urine in a little vial. We would put a tablet into the urine, and using this method we determined the patient's sugar level.

Another procedure that I remember had to do with infusions. In those days nurses, students or registered nurses, were not allowed to start infusions. It was a doctor's task. However, the nurse would have to hold the glass bottle of infusion fluid down when the doctor began the infusion. When we saw the blood return, we would then hang the infusion on the infusion pole. It always took two people, and we were expected to avail ourselves for the task. On one occasion I explained to an intern that I didn't have time to help him get the infusion started. He reported me to the evening supervisor. In later years, hospitals began to have nurses on an infusion (called IV) team and they then took over that task of starting the infusion. Then it became a one-person job.

By October 1, I was assigned to G2, the ward where I would do my surgery care study. On October 1, 1957, I wrote, "First day on G2 with Miss Jones all day. Went to recovery, O.R." My patient for the surgical care study was admitted to G2 on October 3, 1957. "My patient for surgical block admitted to hospital today." The patient was in the hospital five days prior to his surgical procedure on October 8. "Saw my first surgical procedure done. My care study, abdominal perineal resection."

Not all was entirely well as indicated by my diary entry on October 13. "Had a horrible day. Miss Jones fussed at me all day."

But things did get better. On October 14, I recorded, "Lots better day today. Miss Jones better."

One of the last diary entries regarding my G2 experience was on October 16, 1957. "Miss Jones and I had a conference. She said, my observations and principles were good."

The various experiences were progressing rapidly. My next block was rotation to the operating room. All of us students had prior knowledge of student nurses in the operating room. We had to learn strict sterile technique, how to become a circulating and a scrub nurse, and how to cope with the temperaments of the different surgeons. One doctor was known to break scrub and go over to one part of the operating room and pray. Others threw instruments or yelled loudly. We had no choice but to put up with this behavior since each student had to scrub on a prescribed number of major and minor operations in order to pass this rotation.

On October 22, 1957, I wrote, "First day in surgery. Saw cardiac surgery."

185

October 23: "First day to circulate."

October 25: "Had an emergency in surgery. I circulated and Mrs. Brown scrubbed. Stayed up until 4 a.m."

My first day to scrub was November 4. "First day to scrub. I scrubbed on a cholecystectomy for Dr. Ettinger and Dr.Fred Wild was the resident." I remember Dr. Wild, the training resident, complained when Dr. Ettinger left early prior to the completion of the case. That, however, was a common occurrence that the training interns and residents were left to do the final suturing or closing of a surgical incision.

A classmate, Sharon Singerman (Covell) shared one of her surgical experiences with me. "It was my first night 'on call', and I was very nervous to find out what type of case I'd be scrubbing on. Lo and behold, it turned out to be a young man with a serious head injury, and I would be assisting a neurosurgeon who had a reputation for being extremely demanding. When I set up the table for the case, I had to set out drills of all different sizes. The neurosurgeon and the intern 'on call' arrived. The first thing that I recall is the surgeon yelling, 'DON'T SUCK THE DURA!' at the intern who was using a suction to clean up the blood around the head injury. The poor intern was sweating bullets. Then the surgeon turned to me and yelled, 'DRILL'. I looked down at the assorted display of drills and thought, 'Oh my lord, which one do I give him!' I blindly chose one and handed it to him. I waited for him to scream at me for my stupidity. Nothing happened. He used the drill I gave him with no comment. I almost fainted with relief. During the surgery he asked for several things of which I was unsure, and each time he showed me what he wanted. I couldn't believe how really nice and helpful he was. The intern and I both realized that his attitude when he was yelling was out of genuine concern for his patient. After that night I had the utmost respect for the surgeon I had previously feared."

Another classmate, Barbara Byrd (Rome), shared a surgical experience that she witnessed. "Pat Fiedler (Helfrich), fellow classmate, the klutz, knocked the surgery lamp over into the operating table, and she clasped Dr. Cotlar with the towel clips when she was helping him to get his surgical suit closed in the back and the results." Barbara didn't express the results. That is left to our imagination.

We all had a Dr. Cotlar story to tell. He was the same intern who got me into trouble with the evening supervisor for not holding the infusion down for him to start.

It was during the surgery block that I saw my first baby delivered. I recorded on November 5, "Saw first baby delivered."

November 7: "Scrubbed first time by myself."

November 17: "Scrubbed on first c-section. Was for Dr. Miller."

I finally received a compliment, on November 20. "Nothing exciting. Dr. Michel complimented me." Dr. Michel was one of those surgeons we could count on not to yell unlike the reputations of many of the other surgeons. On December 2 I wrote, "Last day in O.R. 95 was my efficiency in O.R."

From surgery no time was wasted. We were next assigned to OB, obstetrics. Obstetrics included the labor and delivery rooms, post-partum, and the nursery. December 3: "First day in OB. Got run out of the room by the mother of a patient." On December 5: "First day Connie, LaRue and I were on OB by ourselves." December 22: "Worked on OB by myself. Saw my care study deliver." We were still on OB January 20, 1958, "Connie and LaRue scrubbed floors on A5." A5 was the delivery unit.

LaRue Storey shared a story about an experience that she had when she was in OB. "I was on OB rotation in the delivery room and Dr. Ball was delivering a baby when he sent me out to get a fallopian tube. I went out and searched and searched, came back and told him I was unable to find any fallopian tubes." You can imagine what a cackling good time those in the know had with this naive student nurse. From that day forward LaRue knew that fallopian tubes were part of the female anatomy.

A classmate, Ann Rex (Denis), also shared one of her experiences on the OB post-partum unit. "One of my first days on the post-partum floor as a student nurse will be etched in my mind always. This was a happy place where women recovered for several days after giving birth. The main job of nursing focused on helping them bathe and placing them on a heat lamp with their legs opened like a grasshopper to ease the pain and help heal their episiotomies, taking their vital signs, passing a few medications, and checking their uterus to make sure it didn't get soggy and bleed. This was done by massaging the top of the uterus with one's hand for several minutes.

"There was a patient in 428 that I had been caring for and had charted 'fundus firm, two finger lengths below umbilicus.' The head of the OB Department, Dr. Golden, asked loudly in the nursing station, 'Who is Ann Rex?' When I answered he asked me to make rounds with him. When we came to his patient's room in 428, he politely asked me if

I had just charted, 'fundus firm' on her. When I answered, 'Yes,' he said, 'That is most interesting as she had a complete hysterectomy yesterday.' He and the patient got a big chuckle out of this, and he had his picture taken with me. Even though I was humiliated at the time, it was a good learning experience, and Dr. Golden and I remained close friends for many years."

## Pediatrics

I have no memorable experiences of my pediatric block. The pediatricians who I remember are Drs. Bertha Wexler, Nathan Kern, Jeanne Hassinger, Suzanne Schaffer, Dr. Simon and Dr. Joseph Diaz, who served as our student nurse Santa Claus. I don't remember any stressful times, and I remember that all of the physicians were very nice. It was not cheerful seeing sick children, but neither was it sad.

One other small memory is that one day I was in the room with a patient and an intern who spoke more Spanish than English. When someone spoke over the intercom, this intern looked up and said, "Who are him anyway." George Orwell had not written 1984 by this time.

## To Vaiden Again

By mid-February 1958, we were finished with the junior year obstetrical block. On February 25, 1958, I left for Vaiden for about one month's vacation. While I was in Vaiden this time, Mother took a short trip to see her sister in Gulfport. In my diary I wrote that mother left on March 9 and she returned home on March 15. I wrote that she had a good time.

## Outpatient Department

I returned to New Orleans on March 23, and on Monday, March 25, my group began their tour of duty in the Out Patient Department—OPD is what it was called—is where Touro has formally maintained a clinic for the indigent since 1886, but the hospital actually provided free indigent care many years prior to that time.

My diary entry dated March 25, 1958 said, "First day in OPD. We went to an evaluation center for the mentally retarded. I'm scared out of my mind."

Miss Anna Engels, our instructor for this six week rotation, made this experience memorable. She was a native of Germany, and to most of us, me included, she seemed like the meanest person we had ever met. My diary entry on March 27, 1958, "Miss Engels was hectic. I asked an aide a question, and she like to have died."

Though Miss Engels had been in this country for years, had gone to nursing school in Rockford, Illinois, and had a B.S. degree from William and Mary College in Richmond, Virginia, the remnants of her native German tongue made her sometimes hard to understand. I would have been too scared to ask her to repeat anything she uttered. One thing that I remember distinctly hearing her say when she was aggravated was, "I'll throw you out the vindow sideways."

On March 28, 1958 I wrote. "Today was a miserable day in OPD. In conference Miss Engels made me cry."

In OPD we were considered public health nurses. The students wore a navy blue uniform with black shoes and hose and so did Miss Engels. We helped in the ob-gyn clinic, the pediatric clinic, including the well-baby clinic, and the clinic for venereal diseases. The VD clinic served patients with gonorrhea and syphilis.

In the obstetrics clinic, we gave instructions to pregnant women about proper diet, vitamins, and the importance of breast feeding, which Miss Engels had an obsession about even in the late 50's. After delivering the baby, mothers came to the gyn clinic for post delivery check. One subject that we focused on was pregnancy prevention, and these ladies were interested, but many came back year after year. This was in 1957 or 1958, and if there were birth control pills in those days, they had not yet gotten to New Orleans, at least not to Touro Clinic patients. But we did tell them about condoms and diaphragms.

Sometimes some of the ladies would claim that they had not had sex and had no idea how they got pregnant. One funny thing that I remember is that we made sure that they understood that one could not get pregnant by sitting on a dirty toilet seat.

The mothers were encouraged to bring the newborns to the pediatric clinic. We would give instructions for care of the baby in the pediatric well baby clinic. On April 3, 1958, I wrote, "Good day in OPD. Well baby instructions better. A letter from Lucretia. To baby sit." In the well baby clinic we would instruct the mothers in the proper diet, when to add cereal, fruit and especially vegetables. We instructed the mothers about the need for vaccines for disease prevention including diphtheria, whooping cough and tetanus. At this time the polio vaccine had not come to New Orleans. I never did see a father present.

Part of our training experience took us into the homes of patients. We were to give instructions regarding care of the baby, the proper diet, etc. I never will forget how surprised I was to find one family in a three-room apartment. There was a bathroom, kitchen and bedroom. The bedroom had a bed and a mattress and the mother and children were sitting on it. There were no sheets or pillows on the bed and not a chair in sight to sit on. I thought I knew the meaning of poor, but poor did not describe this situation. And we were to teach them about a diet high in fruits and vegetables. I was at the impressionable age of eighteen, but my thinking was, "are we crazy?"

In the VD clinic we learned about syphilis and gonorrhea. We never used the term sexually transmitted diseases until much later in the century. The treatment of choice for syphilis and gonorrhea was penicillin. This clinic was a little tricky for an 18-year-old. We treated the patient and had to find out all of the sexual partners that the patients had so they could be told they needed to be treated. This was the tricky part. Often one knew that the patient was not telling the whole truth, but to call a patient a liar would have been unheard of then, or now.

Miss Engels had an obsession with Sigmund Freud's writing. She had lots of books on Freud and psychoanalysis. Many of our afternoons were spent reading her collection of books by or about Freud and all of those stages of psychosexual development, the oral, the anal, phallic, latency, and the genital.

In reading Freud we memorized the defense mechanisms that Freud said were part of our unconscious mind. We were force fed them by Miss Engels. After this tour of duty, we student nurses could explain everyone's behavior or at least we thought so.

Many others had their own memorable experiences with Miss Engels. One of the obstetrician/gynecologist groups during TISON school days was Drs. Weinstein, Kushner, and Cohen. On September 1, 2001, I saw Dr. Herman Cohen. He and his wife, who was Rose Polewoda from Greenwood, Mississippi, and a 1950 graduate of TISON, shared some of their experiences in the OPD with Miss Engels. Dr. Cohen said, "Miss Kessler was a nurse who worked under Miss Engels and was treated like a young lieutenant. Miss Engels was tough and rigid with doctors also, but for some reason she took a liking to me." Dr. Cohen did add that Miss Engels was caring and concerned about each and every one of the patients.

Mrs. Cohen said, "Miss Engels would ask how do you spend your spare time, and a student may say something like, I listen to the radio. Miss Engels would then respond 'you are veak and shows you cannot be alone.'"

Another memorable experience during my student days with Miss Engels was the book she wrote, got published, and force-fed to her students. The Golden Mile by Anna M. Engels was published in 1956 and was dedicated to her students at Touro Infirmary, Past, Present, and Future. The back cover of the book tells about Miss Engels and the front flap tells about the book.

There was not an instructor who lingered in our memory longer than Miss Engels, and we honored her with a special song. The song was "Muddy Water." I only have the words without the music and it goes like this.

I'd rather drink muddy water
And sleep in a hollow log
Than live in Touro's nurses' home
And be treated like a dirty, dirty dog
I'm gonna get me some water
That tastes like cherry wine. Hallelujah!
Cause the water in this nurses' home
It tastes like turpen-turpentine.
I'm gonna go out to Audubon Park
And neck and neck and neck
And tell Miss Engels all about the sexy sex
I'm gonna clean out my locker of
Every little thing I own. Hallelujah!
Gonna clean out my locker of every little thing I own
And tell my mother Hey! Ma! I'm comin' home.

Years later, I learned that this song that all student nurses of my day knew well had a tune like the Jimmie Rodgers tune "T for Texas But we did not yodel. We know today in 2004, we would probably get some serious reprimand or maybe even go to jail if we sang such a song in public.

## Psychiatric Experience

I've written about my medical and surgical experiences, the outpatient department, and obstetrics. My last memorable experience was in the psychiatric department. The first assignment for June, Connie, LaRue, Ann, Sharon and me was to go to DePaul Hospital for our three month rotation with psychiatric patients. We were the first group in our class to go. We took the Magazine bus to get there on our scheduled days. After our block, the next students stayed in a dormitory at DePaul.

The experience was memorable. First of all, it was a Catholic Hospital that was run by the Sisters of Charity. I had likely seen a nun's habit before, but I don't think I had ever talked to one in my life. They wore these big floppy white habits on their heads without a bit of hair showing, and you could only see their faces. They wore a floor-length gathered navy skirt and the top was navy with long sleeves with a white bib and white cuffs. Their shoes were laced black wedge heels. They were nurses, but I surely didn't know nurses wore uniforms like this. These nuns seemed very stern, and I was afraid of them. If they ever smiled, I was too scared to realize it.

At DePaul we were required to attend chapel and pray each and every day. This was probably a good idea, but not a custom of mine.

At DePaul there were various units with different types of patients. Some were acutely ill with psychiatric problems while others were chronically ill. Many of these chronically ill patients had been there for years and would spend the rest of their lives there. Nineteen fifty-eight was a time before the ready availability of psychotropic drugs, though thorozine was beginning to be used.

My most memorable patient experience has to do with electric shock therapy, or EST. The patients dreaded the experience, and I dreaded thinking about it and sitting with them more. In those days they were not given any kind of anti-anxiety drugs prior to the procedure, and they didn't receive a muscle relaxant during the procedure. The patients went in cold turkey and had these electrodes placed on their heads. Literally an electric shock was given and the patient would shake in a convulsion like state when the shock was placed to their head. I was only 18 and by this time I had seen lots on the wards at Touro, but nothing to compare with witnessing this procedure. Electric shock therapy was used for many types of mental illnesses, including depression and schizophrenia. It did seem inhumane. I know the electric shock therapy is still used for depression, but today it is much more humane. Patients receive anti-anxiety medications prior to the procedure, and muscle relaxants are used during the procedure which makes for a much less dreadful procedure.

## Graduation

I did not drift in and out of nursing school. Self-discipline came naturally for me. I only wanted to be a good bedside nurse, and I took my student nurse days seriously. I was generally enthusiastic throughout the three years at Touro Infirmary. Just as I was a conscientious student nurse, I remain conscientious 48 years after entering nursing school.

Many evenings in my student nurse days found me back on the units reviewing the patients' charts to gather extra information, looking up their medications, or studying their diagnoses more closely. I worked hard, studied hard, and on occasions I played. I loved nursing and making a difference in a person's life when they were ill and grieving or when a new baby was born.

We all learned a lot, and we certainly became wiser. We knew that we had to think on our feet, to make quick decisions. We needed strong physical stamina and emotional strength and a good sense of organization. Most of all we must be able to shoulder tremendous responsibility and thrive on other people depending upon us every day.

God's grace was not in vain. We, the student nurses, class of 1959 of the Touro Infirmary School of Nursing, had touched many lives, we had seen babies enter into our world, we had seen and felt pain, and we had comforted the dying and held the dead. These burdens and joys, we shared freely and ungrudgingly and all of these experiences made strong women out of us.

Our finest hour arrived on September 3, 1959, when 22 of the 56 student nurses from the class of 1959 became the noble, bright, shining stars of that class and graduated. All of us now belonged to a Nation of

Caregivers. I had made lifelong friendships. I had fulfilled a childhood dream.

The night of graduation we wore a white uniform for the first time and received a Touro pin to be proudly worn from that day forward. Both the pin and the cap were distinctive marks of nurses and of the school where one graduated.

The pin that we all received was a cherished part of our dress code and within the pin was lots of symbolism. The "Tree of Life" figuratively represents a source of life and vigor. A caduceus, symbol of Greek god of health, is on one side of the tree, and on the other is a lamp symbolic of Florence Nightingale, the founder of modern nursing. The name Touro Infirmary School of Nursing surrounded the pin with the year of graduation at the bottom.

We clutched our diplomas and exited the stage. My accomplishment was written about in my hometown newspaper, *"The Conservative."*

**Touro Infirmary School of Nursing**
**Graduation Exercise September 3, 1959**

We were now graduate nurses, and jobs were bountiful. We could do everything except perhaps cast out demons that crept into our lives or the lives of those around us. All of us had a job waiting for us at Touro or at some other hospital in the city. Nurses were in great demand. We were competent to work any unit—emergency room, operating room, recovery room, delivery room, any medical or surgical floor, psychiatry, pediatrics, the outpatient department—at Touro Infirmary or any other hospital.

As student nurses at the hospital we had covered all of the hospital units during our three year in training. Often times during our training days we staffed a large part of the hospital and we were in charge. There was a house supervisor who was a registered nurse and could be called upon if a problem arose. Today such practice is not allowed.

But for me, New Orleans with-its mystery and magic that I learned to embrace, and Touro Infirmary had gotten into my blood. I felt a tug of duty for a short time, and I stayed at Touro on the obstetrical and gynecological units. However, my preparation at the Touro Infirmary School of Nursing prepared me for any unit at Touro and any other hospital in the city and perhaps in the country.

# Chronology

| | |
|---|---|
| 1956 | Began a three diploma program of nursing at Touro Infirmary School of Nursing on Tuesday September 4, 1956. Fifty-six of us women were in the class. |
| 1957 | Went to a Mardi Gras masquerade party on Saturday March 2, 1957 at Betty Cummins Clark's home. First time heard about mixed drink. |
| 1957 | Received cap in capping exercise on Monday June 3, 1957 at the Touro Infirmary School of Nursing. Thirty-one of the original fifty-six students in the class received cap. |
| 1959 | Graduated from Touro Infirmary School of Nursing on Thursday September 3, 1959. Twenty-two of the original fifty-six graduated. |
| 1962 | Entered Charity Hospital School of Anesthesia in New Orleans, Louisiana in September 1962. |
| 1963 | Met Roger Theodore Graetz M.D.,an intern at Charity Hospital from Sandusky, Ohio and a graduate of Northwestern University School of Medicine, Chicago, Illinois. |
| 1964 | Graduated from Charity Hospital School of Anesthesia on March 10, 1964. |
| 1964 | Married Roger Theodore Graetz on Friday November 20, 1964 at the First Presbyterian Church in New Orleans, Louisiana. |
| 1966 | Moved with Roger to Montgomery, Alabama when he went into the United States Air Force March 1966. |
| 1966 | Moved with Roger to Santa Monica, California in September 1966. |
| 1968 | Eight months pregnant returned with Roger to New Orleans, Louisiana on April 2, 1968. |
| 1968 | First child, Derek Theodore Graetz, was born at Mercy Hospital in New Orleans, Louisiana on Thursday May 2, 1968. |
| 1972 | Second child, Gionne Janel Graetz was born at Mercy Hospital in New Orleans, Louisiana on Thursday January 27, 1972. |
| 1986 | Graduated from the University of New Orleans with a degree in sociology December 20, 1986. |

1987       Received The Outstanding Woman Graduate Award in the College of Liberal Arts from the University of New Orleans on April 27, 1987.

1987       Received the B'nai Brith Award for outstanding volunteer Orleans Parish Public Schools on April 30, 1987.

# Epilogue

In July 2011, I am a retired Registered Nurse. I had worked in the Home Health Department of Touro Infirmary in New Orleans, Louisiana until Hurricane Katrina on August 29, 2005. The hurricane did not actually hit New Orleans, but the rush of the water on Lake Pontchartrain caused the 17th Street Canal to break causing flooding to most of the city. So I decided to retire and devote time to volunteering.

My home had flooded and I had to find another place to live, at least temporarily in Mississippi, my native state.

My plans are to return to New Orleans to live, I hope by the end of 2011.

I must admit that there are unending challenges for a nurse, and the paper work of this modern era saps the energy of the best of us. Sometimes I tremble to think what the future holds because of the paper work, and an enormous amount of government intervention. At times I felt that the wind was in front of me, and I had to push it out of the way rather that having it in back of me urging me onward.

However, the caring, comforting, and compassion of nurses and other health care workers has to remain, and nurses must never let go of them. All have to be given without regard to race, religion, creed, nationality, financial status, sex, or age. If nurses lose their caring, comforting, and compassion we all lose everything.

No other professional person gets to touch a baby when it takes its first breath or hold someone's hand when they take their last breath. There is nothing else like it. We cannot allow acts of kindness fade into oblivion, nor will I have diminished expectations of myself, or others who belong or have belonged to a nation of caregivers.

# Book Review

by Susie James
Greenwood Commonwealth Newspaper
Greenwood, Mississippi

## Graetz: 'A Look into the Rear View Mirror'

**By SUSIE JAMES**
*For the Commonwealth*

VAIDEN — There are elements of a way of life that likely will not come our way again in Carolyn Sue Noah Graetz' homespun, sometimes intense, paperback memoir, "A Look into the Rear View Mirror."

In writing her 213-page book, Graetz repeats genealogical information, linking the life and times of some of her ancestors to events of the wider world. This is a good method that might invite borrowing from any number of amateur genealogists who take the plunge Graetz did and do some version.

Granted, there's a lot Graetz didn't include. During a recent trip from New Orleans, where she's mostly lived since leaving Vaiden for nursing school at the famed Twin Infirmary after high school graduation in 1956, Graetz strongly hinted there's going to be a revised second printing of her current offering, if not a second volume.

Graetz describes growing up in rural Carroll County. Until she was

15, her family's market town was Vaiden, before the family moved into the town in the fall of 1954. In writing about this, Graetz is leaving a legacy for her own descendants as well as to the succeeding generations of other families who might

The daughter of Robert and Dollie Noah, Carolyn Sue Noah Graetz grew up hardscrabble, first in rural communities in southern Carroll County, and then in Vaiden. She shares some of her life's experiences in a memoir, "A Look into the Rear View Mirror." Here, she signs a copy of the trade paperback for a fan.

like to learn how different things were.

In her telling, Graetz often charms, and the reader might enjoy even more anecdotes. This aspect of her writing might inspire an entire "Foxfire"-like series, in fact, with contributions sought from old-timers who grew up plowing mules, walking to the country store, milking cows by hand before catching the school bus weekday mornings, using an outhouse, and making moonshine whisky.

She also sometimes makes for head-scratching, as when she tells about hog-killing time. Maybe Graetz didn't mean to suggest on page 124 that cracklings are the result of boiling the skin of a hog in hot water in the old black iron pot the Noahs used in other aspects of farm life. It's the way she comes off, however.

"The skin of the hog was boiled in hot water in the heavy black iron pot we used for heating water for washing clothes. The resulting boiled cracklings produced our lard. At first the lard was a thick liquid. It solidified. This lard and the ham bones were used to season our turnip greens, string beans, squash, black-eyed peas, and corn on the cob or to fry chicken and everything else that we ate," Graetz recalled.

Cracklings would've come from chunks of hog fat and skin put into that cast iron pot, all right, but without the addition of water. The

*See* **BOOK***, Page 9*

It's good to come home again when you've gotten a book published, Carolyn Sue Noah Graetz discovered recently. Graetz, a native of the Vaiden area, now lives in New Orleans. Graetz, extreme right, chatted with, from left, high school chums Joyce Howard Herod of Carmack, Martha Mann Bailey of McCarley and Margaret Mann Griffin of Vaiden during a booksigning tour in Vaiden.

# Book

Oct 4 2004

*Continued from Page 1*

resulting grease would've been likely enough to pop out onto the people constantly stirring the chunks with long, wooden paddles so they wouldn't burn without mixing grease and water.

The fat and skin chunks did "boil down," and the lard would be strained into containers; the cracklings, reserved and used, too.

While this writer shares much of a way of life gone by, Graetz injects enough of the reality factor, both good and bad, to neutralize sentimentality.

"A Look into the Rear View Mirror," said Vaiden historian Frances "Bud" Welch, "is a cute book."

Graetz also writes about her experiences in nursing school, a world away from Vaiden.

Ida Dunn Alderman of Greenwood, a classmate from Vaiden days, wrote a blurb for Graetz' dust jacket: "I have really enjoyed reading your book. I believe that you can sell a book to half of the people in Carroll County," Alderman said.

Graetz's homegrown publishing house is called "Magnolia$^2$ Press."

"It's because I live in Louisiana, which has magnolia as its state flower, and I'm from Mississippi, which is 'the Magnolia State,'" Graetz said.

# Correspondence

Carolyn—
I'm really enjoying your book. What a gift to the next generations.

The pictures are such fun. I do offer a correction on Page 37. The instrument "outside of the church" is an old fashioned pump organ. Last Sunday night we had our Carol Sing in an old church outside of Pella. It has such an organ which means the player has to have strong legs to pedal the thing — it's a great sound.

Your Chronologies with family & world events really give a good time/place perspective.

Good Work!!!

B

10-1-04

Dear Carolyn, (Sue)

As I read your book, I also was able to take "a look into the rear view mirror." The poignancy of your writing was very touching. I appreciate your obvious zest for life, your honesty and your love of family. Additionally, I admire your bravery and fortitude. It's a long way from Vaiden to New Orleans when you're a teenager seeking a new life.

It took two sittings, but I've read the entire book.

Sincerely,

Phyllis Alford

P.S. James Murry is a little slow (HA), but he's also reading the book.

October 2004

Dear Carolyn,
    What a delightful story -- and I thought I knew you well. It brought back so many of my own child hood memories... especially enjoyed reliving our days at Louro... only wish it was longer— it flowed so well and was over too soon—I wanted more. You are an amazing lady — this is your most amazing accomplishment so far— but who knows what lies ahead.
            Love and miss you,
            Ann

205

Caralyn,

Thank you for your thoughtful
+ compassionate dedication to Numa.
You have offered me great comfort that
his needs are being met.
I'm looking forward to reading
your Book! You are "one in a million."

Sincerely
Christine

Sent: Friday, August 12, 2005 9:07 PM
Subject: your book

Hi Carolyn, Just have to tell you how much I am enjoying your book. I haven't had much time to read so am only about half done....I peeked ahead and I am dissapointed that it stops before you get married....you are going to have to continue and write another one so day...you are so good and interesting. Love, Mary Ann    Say hi to Roger and Gione.

**Subject:** YOUR WONDERFUL BOOK

Hi – I've been sitting here drinking a glass of wine, finishing your book. You did a really terrific job, Carolyn, and should be very very proud. If I were writing a book review, it might go something like this: "An extraordinary job of thorough research, 'A Look into the Rear View Mirror" is much more than just readable: It's a comprehensive account of the girl, and family, called "Noah", and a significant contribution to an understanding of America's past." Thanks!. Gary.

Sent:       Monday, August 01, 2005 11:05 PM
Subject:   Re: my book from Carolyn Noah Graetz

Carolyn, I stayed up until 0230 hrs this morning reading your book and I enjoyed reading about some of the people that I had known of and plan to do more reading tonight. I'll be asking you questions from time to time so hope you don't mind.
     Tell me if you don't mind, I know your folks lived east of Vaiden on what we called the Vaiden - Kilmichael road and am wondering who owned that place ?
     I was familiar with your Dad's drinking and bootleg whiskey making but still though a lot of Mr Robert. None of us are perfect.I can never recall my Dad saying he loved me or never did see me play football there at Vaiden.In Dad's latter years when I'd drop by for a visit we would usual greet each other with a hug and I take him for a ride in the Highway patrol car which he enjoyed.
     I believe most of children that grew up around Vaiden had a lot in common—

July 11, 2005

Dear Carolyn,

    Thank you for sending me a copy of your book. Enclosed is a $15.00 check.

    It has been a pleasure reading your memoirs. It was quite an undertaking, wasn't it! Wishing you continued happiness.

                 Sharon

Sunday afternoon
10/17/04

Dear Sue,

Your book was superb in every way —
I loved it. You did a fantastic job —
your sentence structure and everything
was outstanding. I knew so many
people mentioned and I could relate
to so many of the stories and situations

All your descriptions of your early
life and immediate family was presented
in such an excellent way. Not only was
the genealogy part was so wonderful but
the way you presented the historical
elements was so unusual and interesting.
It didn't take long to read the book
because it was also impossible to put down.
      almost

It was so good seeing you in Vardon and I am
sure your book will be a great success. Can't
wait for the next one

Your and your brothers and sister have
done so well and I am extremely proud of you.

Bonnie sends her congratulations and she
also enjoyed the book.

Excuse this messy writing.

Love,
Aunt Dell

209

2/18/05

Dear Carolyn:

Your Life Story was great!
It's a shame other parents
haven't done something like this.
No, we haven't done it - yet.
I enjoyed!

Tweet

Carolyn's book, "A Look
into the Rear View Mirror"
was so enjoyable to me
because I can recall so
many of the same rural
experiences in my past.

Lorraine Querens

210

Tues Morning

Dear Carolyn Sue,

you made front page in the commonwealth (Greenwood) Paper. Thought you would like to read it.

I have enjoyed reading your book and Dell has really enjoyed it. Maydeen said while she was cooking, the day he bought it, he walked around behind her, reading it to her. ha —

Keep in touch.

Love,
Sessie

# References and Resources

Armstrong, Lynn Stone. 1953. *Golden Memories of Carroll County*

Burnett, Walter Mucklow. 1979. Touro Infirmary

Dufour, Charles L. 1967. *Ten Flags in the Wind. The Story of Louisiana*

*Eye Witness to History*. 1987. Edited by: John Carey

*Gambit Weekly.* May 14, 2002 blake pontchartrain™ New Orleans Know-It-All

Internet www.infoplease.com/ce6/people/A0861783.html

Internet United States History. 1800-1899. World History

O'Neill, Eugene. 1946. *The Ice Man Cometh*

Smith, Gary Michael. 2001. *Publishing for Small Press Runs*

Spence, Linda. 1997. *Legacy: A Step-by-Step Guide to Writing Personal History*

States National Geographic Centennial Edition. 1988. *Historical Atlas of the United State*

*T.I.S.O.N. From Beginning to End*. Compiled by Mary Bertrand R.N.

*The Beginning of Carroll County*. 4/11/1999. As presented to Carroll County Genealogy Society by Judy Stanford

*The Conservative.* April 24, 1997. Special Edition

*The Times Atlas of World History.* 1979. Edited by Geoffrey Barraclough

Thomas, Frank P. 1984. *How to Write the Story of Your Life* Trotter, Sally Stone. *The McEachern Family of Carroll County, Mississippi*

*Vaiden Heritage.* 1975-76. Compiled by Members of the Vaiden Garden Club

www.ingramcontent.com/pod-product-compliance
Lightning Source LLC
Chambersburg PA
CBHW061354280526
45784CB00001B/256